MARY: THE MOTHER OF JESUS

The *Character and Charisma* series
introduces us to people in the Bible
and shows how their lives have much
to teach us today. All the authors in
the series use their communication
skills to lead us through the biblical
record and apply its encouragement
and challenges to our lives today.
Every volume contains an *Index of
Life Issues* to enhance its usefulness
in reference and application.

Other books in the series:

CHARACTER AND CHARISMA SERIES

Mary
The Mother of Jesus

WENDY VIRGO

KINGSWAY PUBLICATIONS
EASTBOURNE

First published 1998
Reprinted 1999

Co-published in South Africa with SCB Publishers
Cornelis Struik House, 80 McKenzie Street
Cape Town 8001, South Africa.
Reg no 04/02203/06

ISBN 0 85476 724 X

Designed and produced by Bookprint Creative Services
P.O. Box 827, BN21 3YJ, England for
KINGSWAY PUBLICATIONS
Lottbridge Drove, Eastbourne, E. Sussex BN23 6NT.
Printed in Great Britain.

Contents

To my husband Terry
who has encouraged, advised and loved me
through the writing of this book and indeed
through 30 happy, exciting and fulfilling
years of marriage.

Preface

Although Mary played perhaps the most central role in the whole plan of salvation except for Jesus Christ himself, the detail about her in the Bible is frustratingly slight. But what we do have is surprisingly revealing. In endeavouring to write about her I have found myself irrevocably drawn to Jesus; in fact it is very difficult to keep on focusing on her, since her whole life points to him!

I have tried not to stray from the biblical text, and where I have used imagination it is to enhance what is there, not contradict it. At one stage I wondered whether I was using too much licence and being over-indulgent in story-telling. Meanwhile, a dear friend was woken in the night while on a ministry trip to India and given a message for me. He had no idea that I was writing a book. He saw me in a vision painting a picture, and was told to give me this message, 'Tell her that the details are important. They help to bring focus to the main subject.' He did not know what the message meant, but faithfully delivered it to my great encouragement!

Perhaps in imagining an encounter between Mary and the *risen* Lord Jesus I have gone beyond the boundaries of certain knowledge, but not, I think, beyond the bounds of possibility or even probability. We do know that Jesus met specifically with other individuals, and that at some point she did see him alive again.

Where I have put words in her mouth they are consistent with things we know she understood and was in sympathy with; or they are echoes of Jesus' own teachings which she may have heard or observed him formulating in his youth.

To me the wonder of her life is that God can come to anyone at any time, break in on their plans, demanding total acceptance of his will, while sweeping them into the biggest plan of all time: the strategy for the redemption of lost and hopeless mankind.

She was the first, but not the last, of highly favoured ladies!

I

Gabriel

Genesis 1; Galatians 4:4; Luke 1:26–38

It was time. From ages immemorial the hosts of heaven had waited for this moment.

They had sung for sheer joy in admiration and wonder as God the Creator had called the universe into being from nothing. Each new day had caused the crowds of celestial onlookers to gasp in awe as planets and stars, mammals and fish, birds and trees and plants and every type of living thing had appeared on the scene fresh from his hand, a glorious extravagant cavalcade of hitherto unthought-of creatures.

In wonder they had watched as God had taken a lump of clay and lovingly shaped and caressed it until another sort of being emerged, lying smooth and beautiful, yet inanimate, upon the earth. He had gazed upon it, this new thing, similar yet so different from his other creations, and there was a look of intense joy and eager longing on his face. Heaven held its breath, sensing that something of unparalleled significance was about to happen. God himself bent down and cupped its face tenderly, and blew long and hard into its nostrils. A shudder went through the body, then the rib-cage heaved. A gasp of air gushed from its mouth, and another was sucked in and the rhythm of breathing became established. Slowly the new creature sat up and looked about him.

God was laughing with satisfaction. 'Man!' he announced. Heaven was fascinated, and even more so when God created a companion called 'Woman', and laughed for joy to see their God so delighted, so enthralled with what he had made. It was plain that the pinnacle, the centre, the all-absorbing focus of his affections was this pair of human beings.

All was happiness, harmony and contentment. The man loved God and loved the woman. The woman loved God and loved the man. God poured his love upon them both. They were friends and nothing came between them.

But a cosmic disturbance took place. The perfection was shattered. There were aspects about the whole affair that even Gabriel did not fully understand. A proud and jealous angelic being, once an inhabitant of heaven itself, had disguised himself as a beautiful creature and deliberately led these two humans, the apples of God's eye, into flagrant rebellion. Pain and loss entered the universe. For ever flawed, it became subject to death and decay; and sin crept into the very heart of mankind.

Heaven was numbed into appalled silence. Even now, Gabriel shuddered at the memory. What happened next eclipsed everything else for sheer unpredictable drama. God's plan was announced. Instead of wiping out the rebels, the Father showed the extent of his love and value for these wayward humans by unfolding a recovery strategy. The Son himself would become one of these men; he would live out the life of unbroken obedience and holy devotion that God had desired from Adam but which Adam had failed to give, and himself pay the death penalty that Adam's race rightfully deserved. In this way he would redeem lost mankind and restore the loving friendship beween God and man and everything that went with it; and at the same time deal with the domination of the evil usurper, Satan.

Preparations began. History unfolded, a chain of events

dotted with clues pointing forward to the coming of the Son. Sometimes the angels were involved as messengers; sometimes they were dispatched to deal with opposition that was blocking the progress of the Plan. Mostly they watched and wondered as God the Holy Spirit moved upon willing individuals, giving them signs and visions and prophetic utterance that pushed the whole thing along. Time, and the Plan, crawled forward, year by year, generation by generation, century by century. The Father alone knew when the fullness of time had come.

But now expectation had gathered momentum until heaven was pulsating with anticipation. The time was near!

Gabriel was summoned.

For the second time in six months, the angel set foot on terra firma. The planet hung in pale insignificance among all the majestic spheres of the heavens. Amidst the infinite magnitude of swirling galaxies scattered like gems of light across the dense black velvet of space, it seemed merely a small crumb; but he knew that in fact the Creator had a special affection for it and had surrounded it with the Milky Way like a setting for the finest jewel, so that people should look up from its surface and wonder at the celestial display and worship the Creator.

The small grey orb loomed larger and larger. It now filled the horizon, becoming luminously blue, wreathed in clouds. Continents were now discernible, craggy mountain ranges, forests and rivers, flood plains and scorching deserts. Gabriel aimed unfalteringly for the Sinai Peninsula. Flying north over the Dead Sea, he followed the meandering Jordan River. The hills of Galilee appeared below in the waning light. Over to his right the Lake shimmered palely in the gathering dusk. Gabriel headed for Nazareth to the west, skirting the dark conical shape of Mount Tabor. Alighting quietly and unobserved, he looked for the small house at the top end of the main street where Hannah and her husband lived. They would be out visiting friends further down the street. But someone else would be there bent over her sewing, working on a very special garment.

'Mary, your father and I are just going down to Sarah and Jacob's house. Do you remember they wanted us to meet their visitors? Are you coming with us?'

Absorbed in her sewing, the young woman momentarily raised her dark head and smiled. 'No, Mother,' she answered. 'If you don't mind, I'd like to stay and work on this tonight. It's cut out now and I want to start sewing it together. Look!' With shining eyes, Mary shook out the long front portion of the dress she had been planning and dreaming about for several weeks. Her mother knew it was her pride and joy, and as she worked on it her thoughts were all on the day when she would wear it – her wedding day. So Mary's father and mother went out and left her to her sewing and her dreams.

As she pictured herself in the wedding dress, poised, radiant, a glowing bride, she tried to imagine the look on her bridegroom's face. The needle flew in and out and her heart beat faster as she thought of the loving admiration in his eyes. She sighed happily. Not long now! In a few months' time she would be Joseph's wife, living contentedly in the house next to the carpenter's shop. How lucky she was!

Her childhood had been happy. Brought up in the loving security of this godly home, her parents had taught her well and wisely. They had joyfully given their consent when Joseph's attentions to their beloved daughter became a solid proposal of marriage, and everything seemed set for a blissful wedding and a rosy future. What more could they want for their daughter than for her to marry a good man with a steady income who lived just down the road?

The last stitch was set in and the thread snipped off. With a sigh of satisfaction, Mary stood up and shook out the folds of the beautiful dress. Its vibrant colours glowed in the lamplight. She held it up against herself and then, laughing softly, twirled round and round. There was a lot of work to do yet, but at least now that it was all tacked together she could see the effect. She could hardly wait to show it off to someone.

There was the sound of a footstep outside the door. It must be her parents returning. 'Mother!' she called excitedly. 'Come and see!'

Someone was in the room. She turned around. It was not her mother or her father. In fact it was someone she had never seen before, and something about him flooded her with sudden fear. There was a brightness about his face that obscured his features and made her tremble. The ordinary little room was filled with an awesome presence. She felt small and insignificant and afraid.

'Greetings, you who are highly favoured! The Lord is with you!' The mellow voice hovered in the warm air.

She was troubled. Why did he address her as if she were some noble woman, someone of high importance? A few minutes ago, she had felt herself to be the happiest girl in the world, favoured and special because the man she loved had chosen her to be his bride. Now some strange, otherworldly being had singled her out and she knew herself to be an ordinary, unpretentious young woman with no ambitions to be anything other than the wife of a carpenter. Panic began to well up within her and she stared at the figure uncertainly.

'Don't be afraid, Mary.' He took a step towards her. She backed and fell into a chair, still clutching her wedding dress. The musical voice began to impart some amazing information: 'God has decided to honour you. You will become pregnant and have a baby boy. You will name him Jesus.'

As the angel Gabriel began to describe this Jesus, he became enraptured. Awe and excitement filled his voice as he went on, 'He will be great! He will be the Son of the Most High God! He will inherit the throne of David; he will reign over the house of Jacob for ever and his kingdom will never end.' It seemed as if he could talk of this King for ever, this wonderful Jesus whose throne-room in the heavens he had just left. His face shone with even greater radiance.

Mary dropped her eyes to the dress in her lap. She could not picture the glory which Gabriel beheld, nor was she aware of the upheaval even now happening in heavenly places at this announcement. All she was conscious of was herself, her inexperienced girl's body, her doubtful capacity to fulfil such a task. Yet in the presence of such a wonderful being, how could she question that he spoke truth?

Falteringly she asked, 'How will this happen? I am still a virgin.'

Again the melodious voice was filled with reverent love as he uttered the next words. 'The Holy Spirit. He will come upon you and accomplish this. You will be in the shadow of the Almighty,' he said, implying that this was the safest and most wonderful place to be. 'So the Holy One to be born will be the Son of God.'

He paused, and as if to reassure her that extraordinary conceptions were perfectly understandable, he told her that her aged, once-barren cousin Elizabeth was now six months pregnant.

'No word of God is without power,' he said and waited. Mary fingered a fold of her dress, but her mind was no longer on her own plans. Every Jewish girl knew that some day the Messiah must come, the Deliverer promised by the ancient prophets. But such thoughts were not remotely part of her thinking that evening; she had simply been pre-occupied with preparations for her own future. Why should she be the one to be the mother of the Messiah? She had earned no right or privilege. Elizabeth, for instance, her cousin, was the daughter of a priest, and the wife of one. Mary could claim no such position.

But the angel had declared her to be 'favoured,' the recipient of divine grace. Later, the Greek gospel writer, Luke, would use the word *kecharitomene* to describe her, literally meaning 'one who is endued with grace' or 'one who has grace poured upon her'. There was nothing inherently in her to make her worthy of such an honour. God had simply picked her out and chosen her to be the central figure in his plan to send the Saviour. Grace – the free, spontaneous, absolute loving-kindness of God towards men – was being offered to her.

Somehow, in the light of this, everything was changed. She saw everything from a different perspective, even herself. She was still Mary, her parents' daughter and Joseph's fiancée, but first of all she was God's woman. He had called her 'favoured', honoured, privileged. She only knew herself to be his handmaid, willingly enslaved to him for whatever he had determined. So be it: she would drop her own plans and gladly offer herself to be part of the greater plan.

She stood up. This angel loved God and served him. This she understood and identified with, for so did she. She smiled. 'I am the handmaid of the Lord,' she said clearly, with quiet confidence. 'Yes – let it be to me as you have said.' She had made her commitment; there was no turning back.

As she made her response of trust and love, new life surged within her. Now Gabriel, whose place was to stand in the presence of God, bowed in wonder. His job was done.

*

Mary is the prototype Christian woman. She was under no illusions about herself, had no expectations of being 'special'. Then one day God broke in on her life and changed it. The angel greeted her as 'highly favoured' which stems from the word we translate as 'grace'. In effect, he was declaring, 'Grace to you . . . you are singled out by God, his favour is on you . . . his honour, his grace is for you.'

That is what happens when the gospel comes to any woman or indeed man. God reveals that he is for you, his face is towards you. Mary was a normal fallible human being chosen by God, for no merit of her own, to bear within her the life of God. The wonderful news of the gospel is that God has life for the world, but he calls women and men to be partners with him in carrying that life.

'How can this be?' we may ask. 'I know what I am. I know my limitations, my lack of experience, my immaturity. I haven't got what it takes to produce life.' Sadly, too many people rightly believe that God does want them to produce a life of goodness, love and kindness but wrongly try very hard to 'birth' it on their own.

They don't ask the question that Mary asked: 'How can this be, since I am but a virgin?' If they did they would get the same answer: 'The Holy Ghost will come upon you.' It is the Holy Spirit who works in us to produce the life of Jesus. It is Jesus whom God is looking for on the earth, not our feeble efforts to make something else out of our barren hearts. We are sterile; we cannot reproduce; by ourselves we can do nothing. But when the Holy Spirit comes upon us, he places the very life of God within us.

So it is with every word which God speaks to us. He always comes to us first with grace, assuring us of his love and favour. Sometimes this troubles us, because we are only too aware of our 'ordinariness'. We don't think of ourselves too much as 'highly favoured ladies' but that, amazingly, is the way God sees us. Then he outlines his plan. Whatever form that plan takes, be it church-planting, praying for a sick neighbour, bringing mercy to oppressed individuals, helping an exhausted friend, giving away money . . . it is always to bring the life of Jesus into the situation, and to promote him. That is what the Holy Spirit has come to do, and what he loves to do.

See how the angel greeted Mary as favoured and blessed, yet in no way promoted her. He talked about Jesus – who he was and what he was coming to do. That is what happens when God comes to us with part of his plan for the world. He excites us and thrills us with the Lord Jesus and then offers us the opportunity to get involved in what he is doing.

Mary was making her plans, good plans, plans to get married. Then God interrupted with his greater plan. She had to lay aside her preferences, her way of doing things, and adopt a whole new way of thinking. That is what God requires of us too. We have to be willing to drop our ideas and embrace what God is initiating, even if it seems impossible and unnatural.

Why should that be? Because when God awakens us from spiritual death to his eternal life, we no longer have the right to dictate our own lives. 'We are not our own.' Mary knew that first of all her allegiance was to God: she was his bond slave. She made her response of submission to his will. It looked like disaster for her marriage, her reputation, her individual dreams. She laid them down, 'died' to them. Yet, as he always does, God restored them all in abundant measure, more than she could have asked or thought.

More than thirty-three years later, the child who came from heaven would be on the threshold of returning to heaven. Like his mother he was utterly secure in who he was. He had received heaven's assessment, his Father's affirmation. 'This is my beloved Son.' Now, knowing that he had come from God and was returning to God, what did he do? Seize the moment to announce his kingship? Declare himself Captain and call out the troops?

He did not produce a sword, or put on armour. He laid aside his garments, took a towel and a bowl of water and proceeded to wash his disciples' feet. His whole life demonstrated several splendid couplets of truth which in human thinking are usually poles apart: King of heaven – servant of all. Son of God – Son of man. Worshipped by angels – friend of sinners.

Highly favoured – bond slave of the Lord.

Like mother, like son.

2

Joseph

Matthew 1:18–25

Joseph was troubled. Mechanically he unlocked his door and pushed it open. He looked around his workshop at the tools, the half-finished tables and chairs and cupboards, the woodshavings on the floor. Listlessly he picked up an awl and stood in the middle of the floor, fruitlessly dropping it from hand to hand. Then with uncharacteristic savagery he dug it into a sawn-off plank. After he had bored several holes in it, he dropped it and paced restlessly round the room. He knew he must continue work on a chest ordered by some new customers from nearby Cana, but his heart was not in it. He went back to the doorway and stared out blindly at the surrounding countryside.

Early yesterday morning Mary, his beloved fiancée, had brought him the worst news that any prospective bride-groom could hear: she was pregnant – but not by him.

He had hastened to meet her, puzzled at the summons, but pleased at the opportunity to see her alone. He had loved her for a long time. He was nearing thirty now and knew he should marry soon. But he had waited, biding his time, observing the attractive girl as she grew from childhood through her teens. Now she was a beautiful young woman and he knew that his were not the only eyes to gaze longingly in her direction.

Her home was not far from his workshop and her way often lay past his door. When he spied her neat figure coming down the pathway he would contrive to be by the window or under the tree outside. He would call out a friendly greeting and they would exchange a few words: nothing profound, but suddenly his day was filled with light and joy.

She was not yet twenty and he seemed so much older, wiser and more mature than she that she did not realise what was happening for a long time; only that she began to look forward to seeing him and sometimes would stop by the open window, inhaling the fragrance of the woodshavings, and watch while he skilfully turned a chair leg on his lathe.

One day he was waiting under the tree as she came down the hill on her way to market. He was holding something in his hands: a small carved box such as a girl might use to keep a necklace in. He held it out to her, and she took it, exclaiming over the carved design on the lid.

'This is beautiful!' she said delightedly. 'All the girls will want one of these. They should sell well!' She was going to hand it back, but he said simply, 'It's for you, Mary.'

She looked up at him quickly and caught such a tender look on his face that her carefree gaiety died away and was replaced by a sudden confusion and breathlessness, and colour flooded her face. Murmuring her thanks, she fled away down the path, hardly knowing what to think.

That day her shopping was unusually haphazard. She forgot to buy the herbs her mother wanted, and bought a small clay pot which she didn't need and behaved in an uncharacteristically dreamy way. She wandered home deep in thought. This was a new discovery and like the delicately beautiful box she wanted to examine it from all angles. Again and again she recalled the tender look in those deep brown eyes and discovered that although surprised, she was by no means resistant. When she slowly entered the house late in the morning her mother looked at her sharply but said nothing, except to ask why she had forgotten the herbs.

A few days later she had occasion to send Mary on another errand. Once again Mary had to go past the carpenter's door. This time she came back singing, carrying a bunch of lilies. 'Where did you find those?' her mother enquired innocently. 'Oh, Joseph Ben Judah has some growing behind his shop,' she replied airily, but the accompanying blush gave her away.

That night Hannah remarked to her astonished husband that he might well be receiving a visit from Joseph and his parents in the near future. When he got used to the idea Mary's father was delighted, and even more so when Joseph formally applied for his daughter's hand in marriage.

So Joseph had entered upon the happiest time in his life so far. He loved Mary and knew she loved him in return. He passed his time busily making furniture for their home together and joyfully anticipating their wedding day.

Then came this day when it seemed that all his dreams hung by a thread, his happiness threatened by a turn of events that no one could have predicted. Mary had been to visit her cousin Elizabeth, who lived some days' journey away in the hills of Judah. He had not seen Mary for about three months, and it seemed a lifetime to the carpenter, who had been counting the days until her return.

He had been working hard to finish a carved chest for the people at Cana and had had to deliver several other completed items to customers in the surrounding Galilean villages. Now he drove his empty cart back along the road to Nazareth, full of longing to see his intended bride again. He recalled her eyes, her hair, her laugh; he thought of her gentleness, her kindness, her modesty and purity, and yearned for the day when she would be his alone. Oh! Did ever a man have such a bride as he? He urged the donkey faster along the road.

As he drew near to Mary's house, she saw him coming and hastened to meet him. She greeted him lovingly and he was welcomed in and shared the family's meal. She chattered happily about her visit with Elizabeth, and the conversation was full of the impending birth of her cousin's baby. Mary's mother was particularly amazed. 'I can hardly believe it!' she exclaimed again and again. 'I do hope she will come through the birth safely. It won't be easy for her at her age!'

'Well, it won't be long now!' Mary said. 'I would have stayed, but she has good friends who will help her. And anyway,' she added, smiling at Joseph, 'I've been away long enough!'

Joseph agreed wholeheartedly. But he noted that she ate little and looked pale. As he was leaving she came with him to the door and whispered that she would come to him very early next morning, just after daybreak.

The grey of dawn was turning to golden glory as he waited for her under the tree. Her hooded figure came quietly down the path and glided up to him. She smiled up into his eyes, but he thought the hand she gave him trembled. Gently he asked, 'Something is troubling you, Mary. What is it?'

Clinging to his hand she gazed at him solemnly. 'Joseph, something amazing happened to me before I went to stay with Elizabeth; but I had to be sure before I could tell you about it. What troubles me is how it will affect you . . . us . . . both of us.' She looked away. 'It is both wonderful and ter- rible.'

He was in suspense. 'Tell me,' he pleaded.

She faced him again. 'Joseph,' she said with a deadly seri- ousness, 'I want you to know that I have never loved anyone but you. I only want . . .' – she paused – 'wanted to be your wife and make you happy. But now something has come from God that is a much bigger plan.'

He was perplexed. What could be bigger than their plans to marry?

Then speaking very slowly and carefully, weighing every word and making sure that he understood, she told him about the angelic visitation. Awe crept into her voice as she described Gabriel, and increased as she repeated word for word what he had said to her. She concluded: 'I realised at that moment that most of all I want to be available to God for his plan, so I said, "Yes, let it be as you have said."'

After a short shocked silence Joseph said, 'And are you . . . pregnant?' He forced the word out. He had to bend his head to catch the whispered reply so that her lips were nearly touching his ear. 'Yes, I think I am – about three months.'

'Oh, Mary.' The words were like a deep groan. He pushed her away from him and the pain in him was so great he could hardly breathe. He stumbled over to the tree and leaned his forehead against the bark.

'Joseph! Joseph!' She clawed urgently at his back. 'You don't believe me when I tell you this is God! Joseph! I am still a virgin!'

Slowly Joseph raised his head and turned his anguished face to her. He tried to speak, but all he could whisper with tears spilling over and running down was, 'Oh, Mary!'

She stood irresolute, not knowing how to reassure him. She felt his pain and longed to comfort him, but felt helpless. Then it came to her that mere human words were insufficient; he needed revelation from God himself to convince him that what she had told him was the truth. She patted his arm. 'I'm going now, Joseph.' She turned and began to walk back up the hill, leaving his forlorn figure leaning against the tree.

Joseph never knew how he got through that day. Turmoil

raged within him as he turned Mary's improbable story over and over in his mind. How could he believe such a fantasy? And how could she expect him to? She must have a pretty low opinion of his intellect. She must think him really gullible if she thought he could be taken in as easily as that.

But then she had always been such a truthful girl. That was the weird part – she seemed to believe it herself. But an angel! Or was it really someone much more sinister who had taken advantage of her naivete and done something unspeakable to her? He clenched his fists as rage engulfed him. Only give him a chance to meet this angel!

And then again, there was this strange occurrence of Elizabeth becoming pregnant long after child-bearing age. Was Mary, young and impressionable, now imagining things as a result of intense conversations with someone older and much admired?

He couldn't settle to anything but tramped around the hills all day in bleak despair. After a while he stopped trying to grapple with how she had become pregnant, and began to think about what to do next. Fear gripped him as he pondered the consequences if – indeed when – her condition were discovered. For the law was quite unequivocal on this point: death by stoning was the penalty if a woman was found to be no longer a virgin before her marriage. True, it was not always carried out these days; loopholes in the law could be employed to circumvent the death penalty. But it was regarded as a breath-takingly serious crime. Not only that, naturally he would be suspected as the one responsible for the pregnancy, and a similar fate awaited him, unless he could convince a jury otherwise. But who was going to believe her story? And besides, he would not want to subject her to public scorn and ridicule – he loved her too much.

But enough to marry her? His upright heart that had so delighted in the prospect of a pure virginal bride was shocked and repelled beyond measure that she appeared to have transgressed God's holy law. By joining himself to her he would make himself unclean. Then he thought about the prophet Hosea; God himself had instructed him to take a harlot for a wife. He shook his head and told himself grimly that only an instruction from God would induce him to do the same. Then Mary's face rose up before him in all its sweetness and innocence, and his heart was wrung. No harlot she. He berated himself for thinking such thoughts. What should he do?

He eventually returned to his family home. His parents were startled at his distraught appearance, and one of his brothers teased him about his gloomy air and attempted to jolly him out of it, but soon gave up. 'A lovers' quarrel probably' was the general opinion, and they left him to it.

All night he wrestled with the dilemma. He cried out to God in his distress. How well he could now identify with David the psalmist! 'My tears have been my food day and night. Oh my God, my soul is cast down within me. All your waves and billows have gone over me . . . Why have you forgotten me?' Was it only yesterday that he had thought himself the luckiest man alive, and was thanking God for such a bride? Well, she was still his betrothed. They were already bound by solemn vows declaring to the world their intention to marry. And he wanted to. But what would be best for her? To marry and then produce a child after only a few months would bring shame on both them and their families. To break the betrothal and leave Mary to face public ridicule alone, with the threat of the ultimate penalty of death by stoning, was unthinkable. Lying on his rumpled bed staring into the black night he shuddered.

Dawn was slowly lighting up the sky as he began to formulate a plan. He got up and leaned at the window. The cool air was a relief to his aching head. Dear sweet Mary! Perhaps the kindest thing to do would be to quietly call off the wedding. This would involve handing her a bill of divorce and settling the matter as quietly and privately as possible. This was infinitely preferable to instituting a lawsuit against her and exposing her to open ridicule. Then maybe she could go away and visit a relative for a while – perhaps her cousin Elizabeth? Yes, and meanwhile he too could take off some-where, just disappear for a while until everyone had forgot-ten they were going to get married.

Now that he had come to a decision some measure of peace returned to him. Quietly he let himself out of the house and went over to the workshop. But when he began to rehearse how he would communicate to Mary – and her parents – what he had decided, that was when he violently drove the awl into the piece of wood. Now he was standing at the door leaning dejectedly on the doorpost. He felt exhausted. He couldn't think any more. Another line from one of King David's psalms came to him: 'For God alone my soul waits in silence. He only is my Rock . . .' He breathed deeply.

The sun was well risen now and the whole valley was bathed in light. He felt its warmth on his face and yawned. He knew he should go in and start work, but first he would snatch a few moments' rest under the tree. Tiredly, he stretched out on the ground in its shade and gazed up at the leaves gently waving in the warm air. His eyes closed. He slept.

Time passed. Merciful sleep refreshed his mind and body. Suddenly, a man was standing there. He was like no man Joseph had ever seen before. There was a brightness about him that was so intense that his features were indistinct. Fear came upon Joseph and he trembled violently. Instinctively he knew that this could only be an angel.

'Joseph, son of David.' The angel knew his name and his

ancestry! The message came with crystal clarity, each word dropping like a gem of light into his dark confusion. 'Do not be afraid to take Mary as your wife. That which is conceived in her is of the Holy Spirit. She will have a son and you, Joseph, will name him Jesus. He will save his people from their sins.' The low mellow voice continued, explaining slowly and precisely what the plan was – in fact what it always had been, as foretold by the prophet Isaiah. This is what the Lord spoke: 'A virgin shall conceive and bear a son and they shall call his name Immanuel: God with us.'

The words were uttered with unquestionable authority and radiant joy. Gradually the brightness faded and the heavenly visitor disappeared. But the word 'Immanuel' hovered in the air like a sweet perfume, filling Joseph with unspeakable, tremulous awe and a deep quiet peace. Slowly he opened his eyes. He sat up, and looked around him questioningly. Where was that man who had been speaking to him? But no one else was near. His heart beating fast, he lay down again and pondered this strange event. 'An angel has visited me,' he told himself. 'God has spoken.' The word 'Immanuel' again impressed itself upon his mind, and he turned over and lay face down in the dust under the tree. Who was he that God should speak with him, a man, a carpenter, confused, troubled, full of doubts and fears? Yet he had; and spoken so directly and specifically into his heart that he could doubt no longer. He could have his Mary. With a clear conscience he could love her, marry her and protect her. Glorious message!

But also awesome revelation. 'That which is conceived in her is of the Holy Spirit.' It was true, then, her improbable story. He had doubted her, thought the worst of her, when all along God had chosen her to bring forth the prophesied Saviour. And he, Joseph, would have the honour of naming him 'Jesus'.

Mary was right. God had a much bigger plan, a plan for the whole world. 'And I am in it,' he thought. The privilege. The honour. The responsibility.

He lay there weakly, consumed with wonder. Gratitude that God had heard and answered his prayers, thankfulness that he could marry Mary, a new surge of love for her, and awe for God's plan to invade human life all mingled together; while around him the air seemed bright with Immanuel.

How long he lay there oblivious as the rest of Nazareth awoke and went about its daily business he did not know. But he did know, when eventually he struggled to his knees, that he would never be the same again.

Mary found him walking unsteadily up the path as she was coming down to meet him. Wordlessly he reached out to her and enfolded her in a fierce embrace. She could feel his heart beating like a sledgehammer, and then, 'Oh, Mary!' But this time it was not a gasp of agony, but a sigh that said, 'Now I know!'

They went back down to his workshop and there he told her that the angel had visited him also with the same message. 'Mary, I'm so sorry that I didn't believe you. But now God has revealed the truth to me and I am so grateful.' He took her hand and looking straight into her eyes said, 'I pledge to you before God that I will love and protect you, and I will honour this child that is coming into our lives and watch over him as God gives me wisdom.'

What do we really know about Joseph? Not very much. We know that he was a carpenter of Nazareth, that he was betrothed to Mary and that he was known to be a good, just man. Betrothal was a very solemn contract, more binding than our modern-day engagement, almost as binding as marriage itself, yet without physical intimacy. As an upright, God-fearing man, he would have put a high value on the sanctity of marriage and would have found the supposed unfaithfulness of his intended bride profoundly shocking and painful. However, we are told that he was very reluctant to expose her to public censure, which indicates that in trying to find some solution to the catastrophic problem of her pregnancy, he was not motivated only by outraged feelings or shock, but by tender consideration for her. He was not a man who acted hastily and angrily. God had chosen a man of patience and integrity, who weighed things carefully before he made decisions.

As he agonised over the dilemma, God spoke to him by sending an angel to him in a dream. He discovered a principle that was to govern his life and which later the great apostle Paul would articulate for every Christian who was to follow: faith comes by hearing a word from God (see Romans 10:17). Revelation from God stilled the turmoil in his mind and brought peace and clarity. Faith has to be acted upon if it is to be effective. Joseph obeyed and took Mary as his wife.

So Joseph also became an integral part of the great plan of salvation. His life too was invaded and turned upside-down. To him was entrusted the enormous responsibility of protecting the vulnerable mother of the Messiah, and of providing the precious child with a safe and loving environment in which to grow to maturity so that he would be able to fulfil his destiny: to be the Saviour of the world.

Joseph has his counterpart in the Old Testament: another Joseph who was also guided by dreams and visions. Perhaps more flamboyant in character, he too was a man of uncompromising integrity. Misunderstood by his brothers he was sold into slavery. He suffered imprisonment rather than cheat on his boss by sleeping with his wife. He was left apparently forgotten in prison, but he refused to give way to bitterness and resentment, and continued to believe in the God who revealed himself and his ways by dreams and visions. He laid down his own ambitions but was eventually entrusted with a mighty responsibility: that of supplying bread for the starving nations of the known world. Perhaps he prefigures his New Testament namesake more profoundly still, for the New Testament Joseph was entrusted with guarding the Bread of Life for the world, laid symbolically in a manger in the little town of Bethlehem, which means 'house of bread'.

Three more times God would communicate with him at critical points by way of a dream. Each time, Joseph unhesitatingly obeyed. He had discovered that when God calls a man or woman into his plan, he unfolds it bit by bit. He also found that there is an enemy who is continually opposing God's plan by seeking to establish his own. Joseph's role as protector of the infant Jesus was crucial, and his prompt obedience to God's instructions to remove him and Mary from the scene of danger thwarted the devil's intentions to stamp out his life and the whole plan of redemption for the world.

You never can tell how far-reaching the implications of obedience will be. 'For this reason the Father loves the Son, because he laid down his life.' There is a peculiar fragrance to God from a life that lays aside its own ambitions and preferences and embraces the Father's will with faith. That is the essence of Christ-likeness that God looks for in each of his own, and in Joseph he found it.

3

Elizabeth

Luke 1:1–25, 39–56

The sun cast a shadow on the wall: a woman's body, grotesquely distorted; a young woman's body, her abdomen bulging with pregnancy. But the only woman in sight was this one, her hair grey, her face lined. She laughed at the strange silhouette on the wall and turned this way and that, enjoying the changing images, her hands caressing the pronounced curve of her belly. Then she carefully lowered herself onto a bench placed by the wall of the house and with a grateful sigh kicked off her shoes.

She eased her aching back against the wall warmed by the sun, and stretching out one of her legs in front of her, she gazed thoughtfully at the foot. Was it her imagination or was it a little swollen? She compared it with the other one. Was it normal to get puffy ankles? But she was thankful that she did not feel so sick any more. At last she could face a plateful of food without feeling acutely nauseous. In fact she was making up for lost time now – her appetite had returned with a vengeance!

A couple of neighbours walking down the street glanced curiously in her direction, and hurried on whispering together. But Elizabeth sat serenely in the sun feeling the child moving within her, waiting. She was expecting a visitor. Her young cousin Mary was coming to stay for a while.

She had been pleased when the message came. She had always been fond of her young cousin. Although there was a wide age difference between them, they had been very close. As a little girl, Mary had been deeply attached to the older woman. Elizabeth was married to Zechariah, a priest, and Mary often used to ask questions about the duties and rituals that his ministry entailed. Elizabeth herself came from the high-priestly line of Aaron and was very well informed with regard to the function of the priesthood. She explained to her young cousin that there were many priests in the kingdom who traced their ancestry and heritage back as far as Aaron himself, the brother of Moses and the first great high priest after the Exodus of Israel from Egypt. In those far-off days, Israel was being formed into a new nation during her wanderings and trials in the desert. Moses received the Law directly from God, and God also revealed the way he wanted to be worshipped. He gave very precise instructions about the nature of the tabernacle, which was a sort of mobile temple, and details about the duties of the priests who were all to come from the tribe of Levi. They were given detailed instructions about how to administer the rituals of the various sacrifices, the rites of purification, and how to look after the sacred utensils. Even their garments were to be carefully made, each item symbolic in its colour and ornamentation.

Of course, the Temple had long since replaced the tabernacle. In fact the present temple was the third one since the one erected by King Solomon. There had been many fluctuations in the course of Israel's relationship with God. Times of disobedience and rebellion had led to chastisement, defeat in battle, even exile; times of shameful apostasy were interspersed with repentance and revival of the ancient ways.

The priesthood had survived, though often weak and corrupt. In fact the religious structure had played an important part in helping the nation maintain its sense of identity during the long years of exile. Now once again the Temple was central to the culture and the priests were a respected class.

Sitting there in the sun, cradling her growing unborn child, Elizabeth recalled the early years of her marriage. She was the daughter of a priest and therefore well fitted to be the wife of a priest, understanding the duties and lifestyle expected of a priest's family. She gave herself happily to serving God in her capacity as Zechariah's wife; he devoted himself humbly to serving God by living an exemplary life in the community as well as in the many duties on feast days and festivals besides the twice-yearly special week of ministry. They became known as 'blameless and righteous', and were regarded with affection and respect by the people they lived among.

Only one thing cast a shadow: why had God not blessed them with children? Their childless state was a cause of great anguish to them both. They yearned to hold sons and daughters in their arms, to watch them grow, to enter that happy society of other mothers and fathers where hopes and fears and anecdotes were freely swapped, and advice and baby clothes shared; to have their home filled with the noise of family; to take quiet pride in each new accomplishment – the first tottering steps, the early days at school, the growth and vigour of adolescence. This was more than enough to fill them with an ever present grief, an ache that nothing could cure. But it was more than that. There was a dark, lurking anxiety, a question-mark poised over their heads, or so it seemed to Elizabeth. Sometimes she had ventured to verbalise it to her husband. 'Why has God not blessed us with a child? What have we done? What have we not done? Is he displeased with us?' The sense of reproach, of shame, was hard to bear.

She knew enough of the Scriptures to know that 'children are a blessing of the Lord; blessed is the man who has his quiver full of them'. They are a 'reward' for the man who fears God. Her husband feared God more than most, so why did he not rejoice in a full quiver of little arrows?

Zechariah too asked these same questions. He would hear his wife's muffled sobs in the night and know that once again her menstrual cycle was tormenting her with visible proof of her barrenness; and as he reached out an enfolding arm to comfort her he would also bleed inwardly with a sad heart. He felt so inadequate to reassure her. In vain he tried stumblingly to convince her that she was blameless, but his efforts were powerless to remove from her the deeply rooted sense of failure. He knew how she would steel herself to join other women with their children in the street or at the well; how their kindly meant words and pitying looks pierced her, along with their whispered speculations, some half audible, although these were mostly the imaginings of her acute sensitivity.

But through it all, she was determined not to allow her personal sense of loss and shame to estrange her from God and spoil her life with bitterness. One of the Psalms often filled her mind and fed her troubled heart: 'Praise the Lord, all you servants of the Lord, who minister by night in the house of the Lord. Lift up your hands in the sanctuary and praise the Lord' (Ps 134:1–2 NIV).

Her husband had often been on duty at night in the Temple and literally found himself lifting his hands in worship as he stood to minister in the night watches. God was worthy to be praised at all hours of the day and night. Was she not also a 'servant of the Lord'? She sometimes felt so engulfed by dark sorrow that even the days were as nighttime to her; but she determined to live them as far as she was able in the Lord's presence. She would not abandon the place of worship.

It was hard when her mother's younger sister got married and had a baby quite quickly and easily. Elizabeth strove valiantly and successfully to overcome her sharp pain of jealousy and longing; so successful was she that although more than thirty years separated her and the little girl in age, a deep love grew between them. Mary was often to be found in her house and Elizabeth felt that the hard edge of her pain was softened as she shared her little cousin's early years.

They had both wept when the time came for Elizabeth and Zechariah to move from the Galilean village to one nearer Jerusalem. It was increasingly apparent that the continual journeys that Zechariah was forced to take to the capital were too demanding. They were enormously time-consuming and exhausting. So they uprooted and went to live in a place in the Judean hills only a few miles from Jerusalem.

Although the two cousins inevitably saw less of each other, their love for each other continued unchanged and Mary managed to stay with Elizabeth from time to time. Each time she came Elizabeth noted with joy her growing beauty, for she was beautiful, with the glow and vitality of youth, the health that is bestowed by an uncomplicated, simple lifestyle and the security of loving and affirming parents. But there was something more – she seemed to carry in herself a deep pool of serenity. To her observant cousin Mary seemed unusually reflective and mature for one so young. Elizabeth felt sure that this pool sprang from a living, vital trust in God.

So the years passed, and eventually Elizabeth had to acknowledge sadly to herself that all hope of bearing a child had gone. She was past the age now, and Zechariah was an old man.

As Elizabeth sat on her bench in the sun, she smiled as she

remembered how one day, six months ago, Zechariah had arrived home in a state of high excitement. The priests served on a roster system. They were divided into twenty-four divisions, and Zechariah was in the eighth, the Abijah division. Each division was on duty twice a year, for one week each time. There were many priests and not enough sacred duties for them all, so lots were cast to see who would perform each function. The one who drew the lot of offering incense in the Holy Place would be regarded as immensely privileged. He would only be allowed to do it once in his life – indeed there would be some who would never receive the privilege.

That day the lot had been cast to see who should offer incense in the division of Abijah and it had fallen upon Zechariah! The elderly couple faced each other, speechless with awe. Elizabeth backed away slightly from her husband, her hand to her mouth. Tomorrow he would go into the Holy Place! Alone! What an honour! What awesome responsibility! She had always known that this was a distinct possibility, but now that it had become a certainty, she trembled with a kind of fear.

That night, Zechariah rehearsed with her each step of the service. At daybreak, designated priests would cleanse the altar and prepare its fire, then a second lot of priests would offer sacrifice and cleanse the candlesticks and the altar of incense. Crowds would be gathering in the outer courts. As a woman, Elizabeth could go no further than the court of the Gentiles, so she could only imagine what was going on. The priest who was to offer the incense went first with his assistants to the altar of burnt offering and placed burning coals from it in a golden bowl, and filled a golden censer with incense. Then they went into the court and struck a large instrument called a magrephah which summoned all the ministering priests to stand in their places. Then the officiating priest would ascend the steps into the Holy Place. Alone there, he would spread the coals on the altar and arrange the incense. Outside, in the Temple court, multitudes were praying, waiting in silence. Inside, at some pre-arranged signal, the priest would offer the incense. As the smoke rose over the Holy Place the silent waiting crowd would fall down before the Lord in worship. It was a moment of intense solemnity, and for the priest perhaps the most awesome of his whole life.

Elizabeth shifted on her seat, remembering. What had happened in there? From her place in the outer court she could discern very little. She remembered hearing the distant clanging of the magrephah and then the quietness of the waiting crowd. She knew that in the men's court they would soon be able to see the first thin column of smoke ascending from the burning incense. In the Gentiles' court they would not be able to see it until it had swollen and drifted up into a cloud, floating and hovering over the Temple.

They had waited and waited; the crowd around her was getting restless. Some of the women nudged each other and whispered questioningly. Eyebrows were raised, shoulders shrugged. What was going on in there?

The priests too were getting worried. After all, Zechariah was an old man; perhaps the drama of the moment had proved too much for him. Perhaps he was ill . . . dead even. Should someone do something? But was it right to investigate? If one of them barged in and unnecessarily interrupted a holy moment what would be the consequences? For it was possible that he was in a trance, having a vision. Unlikely, of course, but not impossible.

As for Elizabeth, a tremulous fear clutched her, making it difficult to breathe. At last, a murmur arose from the men's court and moments later a thin spiralling column of smoke grew and billowed into a cloud. Relief flooded her, overcoming the awe of the occasion and she joined the other worshippers kneeling on the floor.

Of course she did not see Zechariah emerge from the Holy Place, staggering like a drunken man, gesticulating wildly, unable to speak. Somehow, he fulfilled the rest of his duties and then his colleagues got him home, but for several days he lay quietly as one exhausted on his bed.

She smiled to herself as she recalled the most unexpected turn of events that followed. She shut her eyes and savoured the memory. After a day or two, she had softly entered the room and sat beside him on the bed. He had not spoken a word since the day he had offered the incense – indeed, he could not – but now he looked up at her, and such a light was in his eyes that she suddenly felt breathless and young and carefree.

His love flowed out to her unspoken, buoyant, joyous. She had the strangest feeling that if his powers of speech were to return right now he would be laughing. As he pulled her down beside him on the bed, the last coherent thought she had was that he no longer appeared weak and exhausted – quite the opposite in fact.

And now, amazingly, she was pregnant. She who was barren was about to become a mother! She laughed softly for sheer joy and opened her eyes. Her neighbours were coming back up the street. She waved happily and they bustled over at once, delighted to have an opportunity to gossip and marvel over this wondrous event. How was she feeling now? Still sick? Not so bad? Oh, good! Now you must get plenty of rest! You'll have plenty to do later on! Puffy ankles? Oh, I had those too . . . best keep your feet up, as much as you can anyway. And if you need a cradle, we've got a lovely one just sitting there empty . . . Well, let us know. My husband can bring it down if you change your mind . . . Bye now. Take care! And they clattered off importantly. Oh, the deliciousness of being included, of belonging to the gang of mother-hood! 'The Lord has taken away my disgrace!' she exclaimed. 'Blessed be his name!'

But now the shadows were lengthening. Her poor dumb husband would be expecting to eat soon. She stood to her feet and, shading her eyes against the slanting rays of the setting sun, gazed down the road. A slender girl's figure was discernible walking steadily towards her. At the same moment, Mary saw her and hastened her steps. 'Elizabeth!' she called delightedly.

Elizabeth gasped and cried out. For as Mary greeted her, there was a great convulsive movement in her womb, and simultaneously she was flooded with the presence of the Holy Spirit. Light and truth seemed to pour down on her and surge through her, and suddenly she knew things she had never known before with startling clarity. This young woman coming towards her was also pregnant! She had been chosen above all women to be the bearer of the promised Anointed One. This was not just her little cousin Mary – this was the mother of the coming Lord! And Elizabeth knew that her own child had also recognised that he was in the presence of life itself and had somersaulted for joy.

She opened her mouth and exultantly began to declare this revelation. Her neighbours on their way up the street turned in their tracks and hurried back to hear what she was saying. Zechariah, already at the threshold of the door on his way to greet Mary, paused in wonder to hear the stream of prophecy issuing from his wife's lips. 'Blessed are you among women,' she exclaimed, 'and blessed is the child you will bear! But why am I so favoured that the mother of my Lord should come to me? As soon as the sound of your greeting reached my ears, the baby in my womb leaped for joy. Blessed is she who has believed that what the Lord has said to her will be accomplished!'

By now the two women were standing facing each other in the dusty road outside Zechariah's house, surrounded by a little circle of bemused villagers only dimly comprehending what was taking place before their eyes. Elizabeth and Mary looked at each other with shining eyes. Hesitantly, wondering, Elizabeth reached out to embrace her cousin. At her touch, the Spirit of prophecy came upon Mary also and stepping back, she lifted her head and poured out a great declaration of worship and adoration to God: 'My soul glorifies the Lord and my spirit rejoices in God my Saviour, for he has been mindful of the humble state of his servant. From now on all generations will call me blessed, for the Mighty One has done great things for me – holy is his name.'

The stream of thanksgiving continued, rolling out in waves of ever-increasing revelation as the Spirit who loves to glorify the Father and the Son found a willing vehicle through whom to move. The focus was on the mighty God and what his intention had been through all previous generations – to bless all who feared him and served him in humility of heart, by remembering his promises to his people from Abraham onwards.

They stood there transfixed as the influence of the Holy Spirit worked on them by his word. As the majestic phrases came to an end, there was a stillness that could be felt. Then after a few minutes somebody coughed and another bent to pick up her basket, and the little group broke up. Some went on their way vaguely aware that something momentous had just taken place but unsure what it was. One or two were quite uncomprehending and would have been surprised if told that God had just broken in on their lives with blinding revelation. It wasn't in their scheme of things that he would or could do that.

But others never forgot. What they had heard and witnessed in those few minutes profoundly changed them, and made sense of everything that followed. A window had opened in their minds and light had poured in, changing their perspectives on themselves, the universe, life itself.

Later that evening, when Mary was asleep, Elizabeth was talking to her husband about it all. She had enjoyed these last few months sitting with him in the evenings, holding his hand and confiding in him her thoughts and reflections without fear of interruption or contradiction! She sometimes wondered naughtily what it would be like if he were able to speak again. Would she welcome it or miss his silence?

'When I heard Mary's voice,' she was saying, 'and the baby jumped inside me, I suddenly saw so many things clearly. And those wonderful words of Mary's confirmed what I was seeing in my heart. I saw another level of meaning in that psalm I love; you know, the one about standing by night in the house of the Lord?' Zechariah nodded and squeezed her hand.

She went on slowly: 'We have been in darkness for a long time as a nation. God's servants have sought to stay faithful and to praise him even in the dark when we didn't understand. But night is coming to an end. A great light is coming!' The baby lurched within her, and she patted her stomach. 'Some of course will not see it – those who are proud and strong in their own sight. But the poor and humble – it will come to them.'

She turned and faced Zechariah in the semi-darkness. 'All my life begins to make sense. Somehow we are caught up in this great plan. This baby that we are having – of course I know that he is very special and we are especially blessed. That has been obvious all along. But all those years of heartache and sorrow are not wasted. They had to be; they are symbolic of the centuries of night that we as a people have endured; and God is looking for those who will praise him even in the dark. The nation that walked in darkness will see a great light.'

She got up and stretched, yawning. 'Light has come into my darkness,' she said dreamily. 'My disgrace has been taken away. Oh, bless the Lord!'

Zechariah smiled happily to himself. He believed that one day he would be able to tell her properly what had happened when the angel Gabriel had visited him in the Temple. She didn't yet know the half of it! But everything was going according to plan.

Mary lay on the pallet in the small room next to the bedroom occupied by Elizabeth and Zechariah. She was still, her eyes closed, hearing again in her mind and spirit the sonorous sounds of her prophecy flowing out of her mouth like a full and glorious river. Somehow when Elizabeth had cried out her prophetic greeting, it had activated a powerful stream in Mary which gushed up out of her spirit, a sparkling torrent of worship and revelation, full of gems which she had never known or expressed before. Now she knew they originated in God, but had somehow been hidden in her.

She still felt the presence of the Holy Spirit heavy on her. She trembled slightly. Her spirit was enraptured and, whispering, she repeated, 'My soul glorifies the Lord and my spirit rejoices in God my Saviour, for he has been mindful of the humble state of his servant. From now on all generations will call me blessed.'

Wonderingly she pondered those words. The angel Gabriel had called her 'highly favoured' and she had been afraid, not knowing why she should receive such an appellation. That had only been about a week ago. During the several days it had taken to walk here, she had pondered the whole incident. Had it all been some bizarre dream? Had anything really happened? Then Elizabeth had greeted her, confirming for all to hear what no one else knew, and what Mary herself was almost afraid to believe, that she was indeed pregnant with the coming Messiah and blessed above all women.

The enormity of it was just now dawning on her, and she lay on the bed weak with wonder. 'Who am I?' she thought. 'I'm just an ordinary young woman of lowly birth, yet God has singled me out. I'm chosen, selected by God himself! From all women, he chose me! I shall be the mother of the Son of God! I shall change the course of history! Everyone will know how I have been honoured!' It was gloriously, deliciously, wonderfully absurd! She turned over and, burying her face in the pillow, shook with laughter. Excitement was coursing through her. Finding it hard to keep still, she got to her feet, stretched up with her arms and pirouetted around. 'I'm going to be a world-changer! I'm making history! Oh, God! Mighty Holy One! You are doing great things for me!'

She wanted to shout and jump up and down. Instead, mindful of the elderly couple in the next room, she sank down on her knees on the bed, whispering her worship. As happens with prophecy, a window of illumination had opened for her, and she seemed to see how what was happening to her was like a ball beginning to roll through endless generations, a ball of mercy gathering momentum, rolling on and on. How amazing, she thought, that it began with God's mighty arm reaching down and alighting on her! His great finger had come down from heaven and pushed aside those one would have expected him to use – the rich and important, the ruling classes and the aristocracy. It had overlooked princes on their thrones and elevated the humble in heart.

Vividly as through a telescope of immense clarity, she saw all this, that the Great I AM was at work for the future, and in the present affairs of mankind. Now she turned to sweep it back over past generations, as far back as Abraham. Ah! The God of the patriarchs had not forgotten his promises! This great Helper of Israel was fulfilling his word; she was a link in a glorious historic chain. Oh, Faithful God! She lay back on the pillow, at peace in his loving hands.

4

Bethlehem

Luke 2:1–20

Years later, Luke sat by Mary, pen poised over parchment, his gentle stream of questions stirring her memories like fingers turning over gems carefully stored in a treasure chest. No one but she had lifted the lid and pondering, musing, had so intimately relived those momentous days in Bethlehem. Luke, grey himself now and travel-worn from his arduous journeys around the Mediterranean with Paul of Tarsus, waited courteously for this remarkable lady to furnish him with answers. He watched the deeply lined oval face and eyes that seemed to see beyond the hills shimmering in the haze as she reached back into her memories, recalling the events, the people, the feelings.

Wisely, Luke made no attempt to convey the emotions that the events must have evoked. How could he enter into and set down on parchment for all succeeding generations the feelings of a young virginal woman as she gave birth to the Son of God? Or her reactions to the shepherds' tale of angels filling the night sky; or her wonder at the encounter with the aged prophets in the Temple, without exposing her to misunderstanding or censure or even inordinate admiration? Besides, his mission was to focus attention on her son, Jesus. Luke himself was awed and humbled by the very facts that he must record; and cultured, educated man though he undoubtedly was, he felt himself unworthy to put any interpretation on them. The facts could speak for themselves and, wisely, he let them.

So the narrative remained starkly simple, perhaps frustratingly so for us who love to replay in our minds those events which mean most to us. Memories that evoke pain or fear or guilt we seek to blank out; but those we treasure we bring out in the night when we cannot sleep and we lovingly review them, savouring again the ecstasy of falling in love, the fun of a family reunion, the thrill of discovering a longed-for pregnancy. We smile in the darkness as we recall helpless laughter at some witty remark made at the supper table, or a kind and thoughtful gesture. The smell of freshly mown grass, the sound of seagulls, a snatch of song, are powerful reminders of events long past. We preserve the first primitive drawings of our children, photographs of holidays, small mementoes that keep memories alive.

Thus we perfectly understand the statement that Luke makes twice in one chapter, that Mary 'pondered these things in her heart'. How blessedly human! What things did she ponder? Surely, like any woman, sights, smells, voices, replaying in her mind the visual images for ever imprinted there. And surely it was as true for her as it is so strangely true of most women, that we can accurately recall trivial details of an event twenty, thirty years ago – what we ate, what we wore, the songs we sang, the colour of a hat – but what we did yesterday, where we went last week, that seems to have vanished from the record!

I vividly recall the birth of my first baby. How happily I prepared for it. How carefully I laid in a drawer little baby vests and babygro suits, safety pins, shawls and blankets, cotton-wool, baby lotion and soap. How my mother-in-law knitted tiny booties and jackets and discussed with me the merits of carry-cots and prams. She did not at all favour the modern, lightweight buggies designed for a new generation of mothers who had to lift them in and out of cars and did not have spacious hallways in which to keep the big deep-bodied luxurious prams of her day.

I remember how eagerly I anticipated wearing a maternity dress proclaiming my approaching motherhood – and how heartily sick of it I became, since we could only afford one! I read and re-read the little booklet lent by a friend which told me how my baby was developing; and I remember especially the awed thrill I felt when I realised that the tiny flutterings in my abdomen were little human feet and hands kicking and moving.

Five days before I had expected to give birth, I went into labour. I clambered heavily onto the high delivery bed, and looked around. The sheets were white and starched as were the nurses' uniforms. On the oxygen unit by the bed chromium gleamed, and the walls, though old with pipes running across them, were newly painted. The pungent smell of antiseptic prevailed. Everything was clean and orderly.

Contractions came and went and I handled them as I had been taught at the pre-natal classes. When the breathing techniques no longer adequately dealt with the pain, the gas-and-air blessedly relieved it. Often during that long night, I thought incredulously of Mary. How could it be that she went through the pain of birth, the sheer indignity of that most basic of female occupations, the fear that inevitably accompanies a new experience, the struggle, the weariness . . . *in a stable*? In between contractions, somewhat befuddled by the gas for which I was so profoundly grateful, I found myself marvelling, deeply thankful that my birth experience was in an appropriate place, with trained professionals and due attention to hygiene. There was hot water, clean towels and sheets, pain relief, machines monitoring heartbeats, encouragement, reassurance . . . and it was still the most demanding, exhausting, relentlessly agonising process of my entire life up to that point.

Delivering a baby causes you to grow up. Suddenly you identify with every other mother since time began; you now know what it is all about. Your body, once so nicely shaped in a dimly remembered past, is stretched and swollen to accommodate the needs of another human being; then it is poked and prodded, bruised and torn as that human being emerges. But you do not relapse into being a single entity again. You now have the frightening responsibility of caring for this new life. You must protect it, feed it, nurture and train it. You will never be the same carefree, unattached person again; for although the umbilical cord was severed at the birth, emotionally it will not be severed until that child grows to adulthood and is joined to another.

You have joined the age-old club of motherhood.

So, Mary, what were your reminiscences? How did you receive the news that you and Joseph must travel to Bethlehem when your pregnancy was so far advanced?

Mary looked up at her husband, her eyes luminous with apprehension. 'Is there nothing we can do?' she asked anxiously. 'Can we delay going? Or perhaps you could go without me?'

Joseph shook his head and sighed. 'They are adamant. We both have to go, and it must be that week.' He had been talking to the Roman tax official. A decree had gone out from Caesar Augustus himself to every corner of the empire that a census of the population was to be taken and every citizen had to travel to his birthplace to register. Each head of a family was responsible for his wife and children, so as Joseph had been born in Bethlehem, to Bethlehem they must go.

Joseph had taken Mary to be his wife knowing that she was pregnant and peacefully believing that it was through the operation of the Holy Spirit. Nevertheless it was an awesome responsibility to care for her and the embryonic life within her. He would have preferred to keep her quietly at home, rather than trundling around the countryside. However, it could be to their advantage in one way. She was further on in her pregnancy than she looked; first pregnancies are often not obvious for some months when a young woman's muscles are still strong and firm. By now most discerning people could tell she was with child, but probably only she and Joseph knew how far on she really was. So to go away now and have the baby elsewhere could postpone some awkward questions.

For the second time in a few months, Mary prepared to travel south. She and Joseph joined the throngs of people moving around the countryside seeking their place of birth. Some of the time she walked by the donkey, but often she rode on its back as it plodded the eighty or so miles from Nazareth to Bethlehem. They took it gently, finding wayside inns to sleep in along the way. Rather than go through Samaria, they took the route down the Jordan Valley. As they drew towards Jericho, Joseph was pondering whether to go up to the north side of Jerusalem and come to Bethlehem from the northwest, or whether to take the long arduous climbing road from Jericho to the south side of Jerusalem and go through Bethany.

Mary interrupted his musings with a question. 'Joseph? There is another reason why we have to go to Bethlehem, isn't there?'

He stopped in the middle of the dusty track and looked up at her. Then he led the donkey over to a rock at the side of the road and, reaching up, gently lifted her down. Gratefully she sat on the rock while he found the water bottle and unplugged it. 'I've thought about it too,' he said slowly. 'The words keep going round in my head: "But you Bethlehem Ephrathah, though you are little among the villages of Judah, yet out of you shall come the One who shall rule in Israel, Whose goings forth are from everlasting." And it goes on, Mary . . . "Israel shall be abandoned until the time when she who is in labour gives birth . . ."' He took her hand. 'That must be about you, my love! And then there is a lot more about this one becoming a shepherd and his greatness reaching to the ends of the earth. The more you think about it, the bigger it gets.'

They sat there on the rock at the roadside, a pregnant teenager with her young husband, trying to make sense of it all. Were they really the pivot upon which history turned? People drifted by, living out their lives under Roman occupation, oppressed by taxation, by sickness, by their own Judaic Law, all unaware and unsuspecting that Micah's prophecy of a Shepherd Deliverer coming out of Bethlehem spoken centuries before was even now in the process of being fulfilled. What did it all mean? Mary and Joseph were now on their way to bring that child to birth in Bethlehem as foretold. 'It's scary,' said Mary. 'I feel as if we're being swept along in a river of history. It's going faster than I can cope with.'

Joseph put a comforting arm around her shoulders. 'But how wonderful to know that God has planned it all in advance. Nothing will happen that he hasn't already taken care of. We are actually in the middle of unfolding prophecy!'

Mary had good cause to remember his words. On the morning they prepared to leave the last resting-place before tackling the remaining twelve or so miles, she found it hard to clamber up on the donkey's back. She felt heavy and weary and there was a persistent ache in her lower back.

By the time they reached the outskirts of Bethlehem it was

dusk, and Joseph was anxious. Mary's face was white. 'I must stop, Joseph!' she gasped. He was in a dilemma. They must find a room! Night was falling, people were surging around, the streets were crowded. Mary was clearly at the end of her strength. He found a quiet place behind a wall. 'Stay here,' he said. 'I'll run on and find a place to stay and come back for you.'

'Joseph! Please . . . don't be long!' she pleaded urgently. 'I feel . . . .' She pressed her hands to her stomach and bent over. After a few seconds she straightened up and tried to smile. 'It's gone,' she said. 'I'll sit here. But Joseph, don't be long!'

He hurried off and she sat with her back to the wall and shut her eyes. On the other side of the wall crowds hurried by intent on finding rooms. There was much jostling and shouting, tired children crying, cries of exasperation. She slumped down, trying to ease the nagging pain in her back. Then came that strange tightening in her belly again, only this time it lasted a little longer. She could not ignore it; the baby was coming tonight.

She had never felt so helpless, so alone. No woman was there, no mother to support her, no familiar surroundings, not even a bed. 'God help me!' she whispered desperately. She clung to the angel's greeting: 'Highly favoured one! The Lord is with you!' Yes. Even here, in these distressing circumstances, she was still the recipient of God's grace. Peace flowed into her spirit. She was carrying the very life of the Son of God, and he would not leave her now.

Joseph came hurrying back, accompanied by a middle-aged woman. 'Mary! I'm so sorry, the inn is absolutely full, and no one else in the town has room to spare. This is the inn-keeper's mother-in-law. She says we can bed down in a stable behind the inn.' As he was talking he helped her to her feet, but another contraction assailed her. She could not mount the donkey, but between them Joseph and the older woman helped her along past the entrance to the inn with all its bustle and restless activity to a cave behind. A servant had swept it out and shooed a couple of donkeys to the other end. Joseph helped him hang up a blanket to partition it. By now, Mary was past caring.

Joseph looked at the woman who nodded. 'Yes, it'll come tonight,' she said. 'Poor child! I'll come back and help if I can. It won't be the first time or the last!' She helped Mary lie down and arranged a bale of hay behind her, then looked around and shook her head. What a place to give birth in! She herself was torn; the inn was full and her daughter and son-in-law rushed off their feet. They needed her too. Still, she couldn't leave this poor young thing to go through labour without some support. 'I'll send a boy over with a lamp,' she promised, 'and I'll be back as soon as I can.' She bustled off. Joseph got some water and did his best to make Mary comfortable, but what she chiefly needed was his hand to cling to and his reassurance.

The birth was agonising. Mary laboured to push the Son of God out into the world he had made, her nails digging into Joseph's palms with frantic strength. But she was young and supple and vigorous. Mercifully came the last supreme effort and the head emerged, followed by the shoulders. Carefully Joseph took the slippery little boy in his carpenter's hands and gently wiped the mucus from his face and washed the blood off his head. Then he handed the baby, now yelling lustily, to the young mother. While the woman from the inn busied herself dealing with the afterbirth and unrolling the strips of cloth to wrap around the baby, Mary and Joseph gazed at the little round screwed-up face, his skin the typical greyish-purple of the new-born, and wisps of dark hair sticking damply to his head. Joseph smiled. 'His name is Jesus,' he said softly, taking the right granted to him in his dream to name the child – which he would do publicly and officially in due course.

Mary nodded. She didn't know what she had expected, but to her he was utterly beautiful in his soft, vulnerable, human smallness; and her heart surged with love.

The woman came over with the swaddling clothes and gently took the child. She washed him in the bowl she had brought over from the inn, then with practised ease wound the cloths around him and handed him to Joseph. 'Now my dear,' she murmured to Mary, 'you must rest. It's been a long hard night. But first let me make you comfortable.' Exhausted, Mary gladly allowed her to wash her, half-listening to her amiable chatter about how it was only a few weeks since her own daughter had given birth, and Mary would soon be feeling strong again, but for a few days she would feel bruised and aching. She rolled the unresisting young mother over, placed a clean sheet under her, and rolled her back, covering her.

'Now sleep!' she commanded. 'I will come in the morning and see how you're doing.' She looked at Mary's exhausted white face looking up from the floor of the stable, and leaning down kissed her compassionately. Then, patting Joseph on the arm, she left.

Joseph suddenly felt extremely tired. He also needed to sleep. What could he do with the baby? He glanced around. The cattle trough was empty; the baby would be quite safe there. Holding him in the crook of one arm, he pushed the hay into a hollow with the other hand and lined it with a cloth and laid the sleeping babe in it. Joseph lay down next to Mary and closed his eyes.

Just as he was slipping into the first stages of sleep he was startled by a confusion of voices and lights. Clutching a blanket round him, he groped for a lantern and made his way to the door. Mary stirred, but the baby slept on. Shapes appeared through the gloom, and seeing Joseph outlined in the doorway, a small crowd of countrymen came towards him, chattering excitedly. They jostled around the door and one man was pushed forward as a spokesman. He apologised for disturbing them, and then asked, 'I know it's an odd question, but was a baby born here tonight?'

Joseph looked over his shoulder to Mary in the back of the cave, and then at the strangely excited faces of these shepherds. 'Yes,' he said, then added, 'We've laid him in the manger.'

There was a sharp intake of breath, and then the men surged forward into the cave. They saw the feeding trough with the newly born child peacefully sleeping in it and stared transfixed. Then one by one they dropped to their knees. There was utter silence. Mary, watching from the shadows, saw their faces in the lamplight, full of reverent wonder. A tear slid down the wrinkled cheek of one old man. He wiped it away with his sleeve and continued to gaze at the child.

Then the baby stirred and began to cry. Joseph lifted him out of the manger and brought him to Mary. Eagerly she took him and held him close to her breast, gently rocking him and stroking his head. Her shining eyes met those of the old shepherd. 'Tell me what has happened,' she urged him quietly.

Then, prompted and interrupted by the others, he poured out the story of how they were out on the hillside above Bethlehem, guarding the sheep from the predatory wolves and thieves. It was cold and they were wrapped in their cloaks, and talking to keep themselves awake. Suddenly a brilliant light shone in the night sky and an angel stood before them. Transfixed with terror, they heard him call out, 'Don't be afraid! I have good news for you. News of great joy for all people everywhere. Tonight, in this city of David, the Messiah has been born.'

'We were absolutely stunned, petrified, unable to take it in,' went on the old shepherd. 'But the angel went on to say, "You can go and find him. He is wrapped in swaddling clothes and lying in a manger."' He paused. 'We all heard him, didn't we?' he appealed to the others. This unleashed a further flood of excited reminiscences.

After the angel had imparted his incongruous information about the Saviour coming and lying in a manger, the heavens appeared to split open and myriads of angels filled the sky singing of God's glory and his desire to bless mankind.

Dazzled and bemused, they watched and listened. Eventually the glorious sounds diminished and the angels faded from view. For a long time they sat entranced, stupefied with glory. Gradually, they looked at one another and tried to find words to describe what they had seen. 'Did you see . . .?'

'Yes . . . but . . .'

'Why us?'

'Was it really angels?'

'Did you hear the message?'

'The Messiah!'

'Can it really be. . .?'

'What are we waiting for?'

'Let's go!'

Trembling, excited beyond words, they ran down the hillside, jumping over rocks, blundering into trees and bushes, calling to one another. Which street? Which stable? They ran through the streets of the village, looking into one stable after another. Somehow they came to this one and here they were!

'It is just as the angel said,' the old shepherd stated emphatically.

'Yes, yes!' agreed the others. 'Who would have thought he

would be born in a stable! The Messiah in a feeding trough!'
Their wonder turned into mirth and they laughed at the
absurdity of it.

One, a mere lad, who had been gazing at the baby, hesitantly stretched out a hand and touched the tiny foot with
his forefinger. 'What will you call him?' he asked.

Mary answered, 'Jesus,' and a surge of joy went through
her.

They looked at each other. Jesus; Joshua; Deliverer;
Saviour! It sounded right.

One of the shepherds, a family man himself, noticed that
day was dawning. 'Come,' he said to the others. 'Let the
young mother rest now.' And he persuaded them to leave the
little family in peace. But their visit had not gone unnoticed,
for they had not been quiet. Dogs were barking and cocks
crowing and other people came to see what the commotion
was all about; and the story was told all over again about the
angels and the message. So all through the day, a little stream
of people kept coming to see this baby whose birth had been
announced by angels.

Mary thought about the shepherds sometimes as the years
went by. Those same flocks in the fields of Bethlehem were
carefully bred and tended, destined for the sacrificial altar in
the Temple at Jerusalem. They would be led as lambs for
the slaughter, dumb and innocent, slain as an offering for the
sins of guilty men to a holy God. Thirty years later she
remembered those lambs in the fields of Bethlehem when
she heard how her cousin's son, John, was baptising many in
the River Jordan; and when he caught sight of her son, Jesus,
he flung out his hand and pointing to him shouted to the
crowd, 'Behold! The Lamb of God who bears away the sin
of the world!'

Then when on the hills above Capernaum he had taken a

small boy's pathetic little lunch and multiplied it so that five thousand people had enough to eat, she thought about how so small a person as a baby could grow in the hands of God and become bread for soul-hungry millions.

She remembered too when he proclaimed to a crowd starved of reality and truth, hungry for God, 'I am the Bread of Life. He who comes to me shall never hunger,' that he had been laid in a manger in Bethlehem which means 'House of Bread'.

And right at the end when he had broken bread and given it to his disciples and said, 'This is my body broken for you; do this and remember me,' she remembered how Joseph had taken that tiny little body and laid it in a feeding trough, not knowing then that what he did was a symbol for all mankind in all the world.

5

Simeon and Anna

Luke 2:21–38

After a few days, the crowds in Bethlehem thinned out and the little town resumed its placid existence. Joseph found a small empty house to rent and moved Mary and Jesus into it. She was beginning to feel stronger now. On the eighth day, Joseph went to the synagogue and came back with the chief rabbi, who performed the ritual circumcision, and the child was formally named 'Jesus', just as the angel had said before he was conceived.

Dusk was falling and the evening shadows lengthening. Mary's eyes were closed. Luke wondered if she were hearing again the angel's voice saying, 'He shall be called Jesus, for he shall save his people from their sins,' or the voice of the rabbi proclaiming, 'His name is Yeshua!' and the shrill squeal of pain from the baby as he took the knife and severed the tiny scrap of flesh.

Luke did not want to disturb her reverie but time was short. He must get down as much as he could, and write it out in an orderly fashion for his friend Theophilus, a noble and influential Roman who was expressing great interest in the origins of the Christian faith now fast spreading throughout the civilised nations around the Mediterranean.

He had promised that he would carefully investigate everything that had happened to Jesus from the beginning. Luke also had a shrewd idea that his writings would be an important source of information for many people beyond Theophilus.

Jesus was born into a Jewish home and brought up according to the Law by his devout parents. So Luke faithfully recorded that he was circumcised; but also as the firstborn he had to be consecrated to God. For forty days after the birth, Mary was considered to be ritually unclean. When those days were completed, Joseph took her to the Temple. Before entering the Temple precincts, she first immersed herself in the *mikveh*, the ritual cleansing bath, and then entered the court of women. There she placed money for her purification sacrifice in a horn-shaped container presided over by a priest. Then she, and other women in the same situation, gathered on a platform overlooking the courtyard where the animals purchased with the money were sacrificed. That done, she and Joseph could attend to the redemption of the first-born.

Every first-born son not born to a Levite had to be redeemed or 'bought back' at one month old. Parents had to take the child either to a local priest or to the Temple. Bethlehem was not far from Jerusalem, so it was convenient for Mary and Joseph to combine her purification with Jesus' redemption. For five shekels they purchased a pair of pigeons, which were then sacrificed by the priest.

'So you took Jesus to the Temple,' Luke prompted gently.

Mary opened her eyes again and sat up. 'Oh yes! Then something else happened that was amazing. In fact, it helped me understand a lot of things that took place years later.'

Simeon had woken earlier than usual that morning. Stiffly, slowly, he rose up from his bed and stood in the shaft of sunlight coming through the high window. Lifting his head he intoned softly, 'Blessed art thou, O Lord our God, King of the universe,' and went on to recite the prayers that he had used all his life. But for Simeon this was no hurried ritual; he meant every word.

Now that he was old and frail he had more time to reflect, and lately he had sensed within himself an expectation, a waiting for something to happen. He meditated much on certain scriptures about light dawning in darkness. Grieving over the occupation of his nation by mighty Rome, he prayed for deliverance, and his prayers focused increasingly on the need for a Deliverer. Sometimes when he awoke in the night his mind would dwell on prophecies concerning a Saviour, One who would spring from the root of Jesse, a son of David whose kingdom would never end. A yearning grew in his heart. He could not remember precisely when it began, but he became expectant that he himself would behold this Saviour with his own eyes.

Naturally all Jews were conversant with these same prophetic scriptures; but on the whole, when he discussed them with others, he found few, if any, who believed in their imminent fulfilment. Oh yes, they believed that one day in the distant future they would come to pass, but for now they were preoccupied with the complications of preserving the traditional ways of life and the dictates of the Law while living under Roman jurisdiction. Simeon was regarded as righteous and devout but a bit obsessive. But although others might smile, thinking his obsession merely the fancy of an old man, he did not let go of his conviction. The Saviour would come and he would see him!

It was a day like any other. Crowds thronged the streets, buying and selling; beggars rattled a few coins in their begging bowls, calling querulously for alms; here and there, groups of people squatted in the shade of date palms chatting or dozing; bags of merchandise were unloaded from camels; women exchanged news and called after mis-behaving children, and all the while a steady stream of traffic passed in and out of the Temple courts.

Simeon puffed his way up the narrow street as fast as his tired old legs would let him, making good use of his staff to stop and lean on every now and then and catch his breath. More than once he shook his head. 'What am I doing this for?' he murmured. 'I've no particular reason to be in the Temple today.' Yet he acknowledged a stirring within, a strange compulsion drawing him onwards. He was not unfa-miliar with this inner urge; it was the gentle but insistent tug of the Holy Spirit, whose voice he had learned to identify. In fact it was the very one who had been revealing to him for a long time now that he would have his heart's desire. The light, the desire of nations, would come suddenly to his Temple, and before death closed his eyes he would see the Christ. But how would he recognise him? What would he look like? He had no idea.

Now his heart beat with a joyous excitement. Why, he did not know. He felt the Holy Spirit all over him, enveloping him, and found himself whispering happily, 'Yes, Lord, I'm coming, I'm coming!' He passed into the Temple courts, past the goats and lambs tethered waiting to be purchased, past the money-changers in the court of the Gentiles.

He paused. The general bustle of activity flowed around him, but he stood still, an island of expectancy, oblivious to everything except the heavy presence of the Spirit. His atten-tion was riveted to a young couple with a baby, threading their way towards the altar. He watched as they approached the officiating priest. Then slowly, deliberately as if in a dream, he walked towards them. The young husband handed over two pigeons to the priest who expertly dis-patched them and offered them on the altar.

Mary and Joseph turned as if to leave, but their way was blocked. Mary raised her eyes and looked into the face of the old man. Unfathomable longing was in his eyes as, speechlessly, he gazed at her and held out his arms. Silently, she put the infant Jesus into them. His eyes devoured the face of the child and filled with tears.

Concerned, Joseph and Mary looked at each other, and Joseph put a friendly hand on his shoulder as if to steady him. Smiling, the tears now running freely down the wrinkles, Simeon shook his head, trying to reassure them. Then, taking a deep breath, he lifted up the baby in his arms and flung back his head. Passers-by were startled to hear his deep voice praying exultantly: 'Sovereign Lord . . . you may now dismiss your servant in peace. For my eyes have seen your salvation, which you have prepared in the sight of all people, a light for revelation to the Gentiles and for glory to your people Israel.'

His face was radiant as he handed the baby back to his mother. Amazed, Mary and Joseph looked at each other in wonder and bowed their heads. Simeon laid his hands on them and blessed them. Then, still moved by the Holy Spirit, he prophesied over Mary.

They were enigmatic words – not words she would have chosen to hear. Up to now every word she had heard about her son had been positive: Gabriel's announcement, Elizabeth's utterance, the message of the angels to the shepherds – all had spoken of the promised Messiah being one who would bring good news, peace on earth, salvation.

Now a new note was introduced. Not all would receive this child with unmitigated joy. 'This child is destined to cause the falling and rising of many in Israel, and to be a sign that will be spoken against . . . the thoughts of many hearts will be revealed. And a sword will pierce your own heart too.' Not words of comfort and joy, but words to ponder; and later she did. But right now her attention was diverted by another elderly person approaching – this time a woman.

She was quite well known in the Temple precincts: a diminutive, wrinkled old widow named Anna. She had been around in the Temple as long as anyone could remember, and was regarded almost as part of the furniture. 'Who is she?' visitors would ask as the bent figure in black shuffled her way around, tapping with her stick on the marble flagstones. 'Oh, that's Anna,' they would be told. 'Her father was Phanuel from the tribe of Asher.'

'Why is she here?'

'Well, apparently she was married for seven years and then her husband died and she had no other family. So she just sort of stayed around here. How old? Well, someone told me that she is about eighty-four. Yes, *very* old, isn't it? No, I don't think she eats very much, but they say she prays a lot. Yes, she is quite a character – a prophetess some say.'

Anna shuffled up now and elbowed her way through the little group that was forming around Mary and Joseph and Simeon. Unabashedly she poked Simeon with her stick, and pushed through to the centre, staring with bright fascinated eyes at the baby in Mary's arms. Suddenly he opened his eyes and sneezed, and smiled sleepily.

'He's the one!' she wheezed delightedly. She put out a knobbly arthritic finger and stroked him gently, then looked up at Mary and Joseph, both a bit dazed by now, and saw the tears on Simeon's face. Grinning hugely, she nodded wisely. 'Yes, you know, don't you? Well, thanks be to God!' She turned to the assembled throng and repeated emphatically, 'Thanks be to God! This is the one we've been waiting for! Yes, this child is destined to be our Redeemer! His parents brought him here today to be redeemed as their first-born son. But I tell you he shall be the Redeemer!' Her lined old face was alight with joy and from that moment on, her few remaining days were no longer filled with fasting and pain, but with a vast peace and contentment. He had come, the Saviour of the world! And she told anyone who would listen.

Simeon could not remember how he got home. Somehow, he retraced his steps, blindly, automatically, his feet carrying him, but his mind far away, his spirit in ecstasy. He arrived at his house and stood stupidly in front of the door. He did not want to go in and get swallowed up in life's routine just yet. He wanted to savour, to prolong, this wonderful day. He wandered a little further up the twisty street and came to a stone seat set in a wall overlooking part of the city. Suddenly engulfed by a wave of tiredness, he sank down onto it and closed his eyes.

Immediately before him rose the vision of the face of the child resting so peacefully in his arms; and again a sob welled up from deep within him. 'I have seen him!' he murmured brokenly. 'I have touched and handled and beheld with my own eyes the Light of the nations! Oh, glory to God!' Weak with wonder, he sat on until daylight faded and the lights began to appear in the streets below.

How well he would have identified with the words of the apostle John, decades later, who wrote a letter to encourage and strengthen believers beleaguered by gnostic thinking. The importance of the incarnation was being belittled and a new so-called 'higher knowledge' was being propagated, emphasising mystical concepts and down-playing that Jesus was truly human, a man of flesh and blood. So John wrote robustly, 'That which . . . we have seen with our eyes, which we have looked at and our hands have touched – this we proclaim concerning the Word of life . . . We write this to make our joy complete. This is the message, . . . God is Light . . .' (1 John 1:1, 4 NIV).

Simeon's joy was so complete he could hardly contain it.

*

Mary turned her expressive eyes towards Luke and smiled at him. 'Do you know,' she said, 'I heard that neither Simeon nor Anna lived much longer after that. In fact, Zechariah, my cousin Elizabeth's husband, knew Simeon quite well. He took his own little boy, John, who was about eight months old, to visit Simeon not long after. Apparently Simeon took one look at John and launched into an account of his meeting with us in the Temple.' She paused, thinking about those two old men talking and sharing their prophetic insights, and laughed. 'Imagine them both getting so excited over two baby boys!'

'But the similarity of their prophecies is so striking!' exclaimed Luke eagerly. He had already researched the story of John's birth. He recalled now that at John's circumcision the dumb Zechariah's tongue had suddenly been loosened to declare a prophecy. His son John would be a prophet of the Most High, a forerunner 'to prepare the way for him who would come as the rising sun from heaven, to shine on those living in darkness and the shadow of death, and guide their feet into the way of peace'. And now Simeon had proclaimed over Jesus that he was 'a light for revelation to the Gentiles and for glory to . . . Israel'.

'Do you think either of them had any idea what they were talking about?' Luke asked Mary.

'Do you mean Zechariah and Simeon?' she replied. 'Yes, they brought remarkable prophecies, didn't they? And yet as I have pondered on that day, I have realised also that the whole of Anna's life was prophetic. Prophecy is not always only verbal. She made a profound declaration by her very lifestyle.'

'Please go on!' said Luke, fascinated.

'Just think! She had such a passionate longing to see the coming Messiah that it shaped her whole life. She fasted and prayed in the Temple for decades – probably over sixty years.

What faith! What devotion! And how God honoured that yearning by giving her a special glimpse of his glory. She saw so little, Luke. She was consumed with a vision all her life; and God granted her a few moments with a tiny baby. She never saw him grow up, or heard him teach, or heal lepers, or give blind men their sight. She did not witness his death and resurrection. Her hopes were based on God's promises in the ancient Scriptures. But they were enough to plant in her an all-consuming yearning for him.'

While Mary was speaking, Luke was drawn back irresistibly to hearing Paul dictate in his letter to Timothy, with the same expectancy and eager longing, 'There is laid up for me a crown of righteousness which the Lord will award me on that day; and not only to me, but to all those who passionately look for his coming.' Anna knew so little but loved so much. Should he, looking back from the other side of the cross with so much more understanding, watch and long for him less? He understood why Mary had said that Anna's life was prophetic: it pointed forward to more truth than she knew.

Mary spoke out of her own experience and her own heart. 'Prophecy never originates in the will of man. Men speak from God as they are carried along by the Holy Spirit.' She was quiet for a while, searching for words. 'When the Holy Spirit comes upon you, there is a deep knowing that goes beyond human understanding. You know dimly at the time that the words you say and the things you do when he overshadows you have a huge significance beyond the present moment.'

No one knew more supremely than Mary the experience of the Word being birthed in her by the Holy Spirit. For her at the time it had been acquiescence to a vast eternal plan, a seed planted, a tiny baby. Now with hindsight and foresight she understood more of the cosmic implications.

Luke nodded in agreement. He had travelled all over the Mediterranean with the apostle Paul. He had heard him give his story of conversion many times – the story of how he had seen a great light as he travelled on the road to Damascus and a voice commissioning him: 'I am sending you to the Gentiles to open their eyes and turn them from darkness to light and from the power of Satan to God so that they might receive forgiveness of sins.'

How amazing was the consistency of these prophetic words! He knew enough of Jewish literature to know that Isaiah had foreseen centuries before one who would come as a light, springing from Abraham's stock, and yet whose rays would spread beyond Israel to the Gentiles. How immense was the scope of God's plan of salvation in the person of Jesus Christ!

And Luke – the Greek, the Gentile, the Christian – bowed his head in awe and thankfulness. 'I am part of it,' he thought, 'for the light reached even to me.'

6

The Astronomers

Matthew 2:1–12

One evening, when Jesus was nearly a year old, Joseph was making his way back home with his donkey and cart from the market-place in Bethlehem. He had been selling the plough handles, yokes, tools and household implements which he made to support his family. Mary had slipped into her role of mothering her little son, and they had settled into a fairly comfortable routine. They had decided to stay on in this small town, having no particular reason to hurry back to Nazareth.

For several evenings a star of unusual brilliance had dominated the night sky. Joseph passed clusters of people standing around their doorways or in the streets, gazing up into the night and exclaiming at its astonishing brightness. Some said it was a comet; others insisted it was a sign, an omen of some significant event, but were vague when pressed as to what that might be.

Now as Joseph led the donkey through the maze of little streets, the star hung low on the horizon, just above the ridge where his home was. It was a clear night and the star was so bright that it outshone the palely rising moon and cast a shadow behind him.

Towards the edge of the town, he passed the inn. Quite a

stir was going on in there tonight! He stood still by the gateway and watched, fascinated by all the activity going on in the courtyard. A train of camels had arrived and was being unloaded. Joseph smiled to himself as he saw the inn-keeper rubbing his hands and bowing deferentially to a tall commanding figure in a flowing crimson robe and plumed turban. A jewel flashed in the folds of silk, and another on his hand as he reached for a goblet of wine.

A thick-set bearded man was piling up leather bags and sacks in the centre of the courtyard by the well, and two more, bare to the waist, clad in loose baggy trousers, staggered under the weight of an ornate carved chest. Others were busy watering camels, and servants were moving around carrying food and bedding. From an upstairs room came convivial sounds of talking and laughter, eating and drinking.

Joseph resumed his journey, looking forward to telling Mary about the strange travellers. He wondered what they were doing in this small town. Merchants usually went by the coastal route or up the Jordan Valley. Although not far from Jerusalem, Bethlehem was slightly off the commercial route and the little inn would once again be stretched to its limits to accommodate this camel train.

Behind the inn he stopped again, but this time in sheer wonder at the breathtaking brilliance of the star. As he climbed the small hill, it seemed to him that he was walking towards it. The words of Isaiah's prophecy came to mind: 'The people who walked in darkness have seen a great light.' He reached the house and stood for a moment, his hand on the door-latch, and looked down over the valley bathed in the light of the amazing star.

The lights down at the inn were dull by comparison. Noise floated up to him: snatches of laughter, the jingle of harnesses, the yapping of dogs and general hubbub. He turned and opened the door and went in.

The lamplight lit a serene picture. Mary was playing with Jesus, bouncing him up and down on her lap, and he was laughing and shrieking with delight. On the table nearby lay bread fragrantly new, and from an earthenware pot issued an appetising aroma. Joseph sighed contentedly. How far removed it seemed from the clamour of the inn down the hill! He sat down and as Mary ladled stew into a dish he began to tell her about the strange travellers.

'Camels!' exclaimed Mary. 'How many?'

'I couldn't be sure,' said Joseph, 'but they had very ornate bridles. There seemed to be a lot of people scurrying about, and some were unloading bags and chests.'

'Merchants, I suppose,' said Mary. 'Probably bringing spices and things to Egypt.'

'But why come this way? Why not stay in Jerusalem or Jericho? I mean, there won't be many customers here!'

Mary laughed. 'Imagine it! Persian rugs! Alabaster pots full of liquid myrrh!' She put Jesus down gently on the floor on a rug. Then speaking imperiously to an imaginary flunky, she pointed to piles of imaginary merchandise. 'Remove these to my palace immediately! I shall decide on the carpets later when the marble floors are finished.' Joining in the pretence, Joseph snatched up a broom. 'My lady, the night is warm. Allow me to fan you!'

Giggling together, they did not at first hear the commotion outside. Then hearing shouts, Joseph opened the door and stood in astonished surprise. On the threshold stood a stranger, his dark bearded face shadowed by a turban. He bowed, and behind him in the light of the luminous star Joseph could see a small crowd of people and some camels – the party of travellers he had seen at the inn!

Mary snatched up Jesus and sat down with him, holding him tightly. Then, as if in a dream, she saw the first man point at the child and turn and shout something to the people behind him. Suddenly the tiny house was full of foreign men, pressing in and bowing before her. They squeezed in and prostrated themselves, their heads on the floor, their voices hushed and awed. Outside the open door starlight poured down, bathing the valley in its radiant light.

An elderly man raised his head and looked at her little son with tender eyes. Chuckling, the child grabbed at his beard. The man caught hold of the little hand and kissed it, murmuring words in a tongue that neither Mary nor Joseph understood. They glanced at each other bemused. Then the first man who had knocked at the door began to speak to Joseph in Aramaic.

Mary listened in wonder as his story unfolded. It appeared that he was the trusted steward of one of these men and through much travelling had picked up enough Aramaic to make himself understood. He pointed to the imposing grey-headed man at present kneeling before Jesus. This was his master, Balthasar, a nobleman renowned for his wisdom and learning. He and his like-minded companions spent time charting the movement of stars and planets. With much gesticulation he gave Mary and Joseph to understand how they had noticed the arrival of a hitherto unknown celestial body. Its position and the way it appeared to increase in brightness caused them to believe it had special significance. It seemed to move across the heavens in a south-westerly direction. After plotting its course and consulting various tomes of prophecies and omens they decided to follow it.

There was a slight interruption here as the astronomer spoke with his steward in his own tongue. 'He wants me to explain that they believe the appearance of the star portends the birth of a great King who will arise among the Jews.'

The steward put his hand on Joseph's shoulder and spoke confidentially: 'You know, my friend, as you travel around from Persia to Mesopotamia, through Aram to Egypt, you bump into people; you get to hear stories, rumours. People tell you their dreams and longings. Every once in a while you meet a humble man in a desert somewhere who has more than dreams; he has . . . ah, revelations. Prophecies of a Messiah arising from the Jews are not unknown.'

This was no surprise to Mary and Joseph. Many of these prophecies had been given in the days before or during the Exile period in Babylon. Jews who had chosen not to return to their native land must have clung to those prophecies, just as they clung to their traditions and culture to preserve their distinctive identity in an alien land. But they marvelled that these learned astronomers should take so seriously the Scriptures they had read and link them so specifically with the flaming star which had led them here. They must have been deeply convinced about the importance and veracity of their quest to make such a long and hazardous journey lasting many months.

Mary noticed a thin man in a blue robe standing in the shadows near the door. He was bare-headed save for a thin silver circlet. His piercing eyes, deep set in an intelligent face, appeared to miss nothing. Now he raised a commanding hand and beckoned the steward. He spoke a few soft phrases. 'Yes, my Lord Melchior,' responded the steward, and he went out of the door, reappearing a few minutes later with a scroll which he handed to the thin man with a bow.

Slowly and deliberately, Melchior crossed the room. Others parted and made space for him as he knelt on the floor and unrolled the scroll. He spread it out and read in Hebrew words familiar to Mary and Joseph: 'Arise, shine for your light has come and the glory of the Lord rises upon you. Behold darkness covers the earth and gross darkness the people but the Lord rises on you. Nations shall come to your light and kings to the brightness of your dawn.'

He stood up and addressed Mary and Joseph. 'Where I

come from, I am like a king,' he stated in fluent Aramaic. 'I give orders, I am obeyed. But as one gazes at the sky night after night, one becomes very aware of one's fragility and insignificance, and a deep longing grows within to honour and worship a greater King, the source of light and life. All of my life I have sought such a King! I have read, I have pondered and questioned. And now I have been led here.'

He paused and looked around at the strange assortment of rich and poor in the ordinary drab little house and jabbed with his forefinger at the words on the parchment. 'This is the dawn!' he exclaimed. 'This child – he is the one, the light, the dayspring. Somehow I know . . . I believe . . .' His voice trailed off. He turned back and faced Jesus sitting on Mary's knee. Silence filled the room.

The little boy was absolutely still. Mary watched Melchior's ascetic face and saw his dark restless eyes change as comprehension flooded his soul. 'I worship you,' he said.

Something broke. He was on the floor, face down. His muffled voice repeated, 'I worship you, I worship you.' A wave of glory seemed to fill the room and again all were on their knees. Mary stared with wonder at the awesome sight of these rich, powerful, knowledgeable men bowing before her son. No words broke the silence that settled like a cloud over them. Then gradually a ripple of sound began, at first just murmured whisperings like the wind ruffling through long grass, then increasing until loud exclamations of adulation mingled with shouts of joy.

At length Melchior raised his head. The strained look had left his face to be replaced by a kind of carefree happiness. Where had she seen that look before? Instantly, the faces of the shepherds rose in her memory, and those of Simeon and Anna. She was in a unique position to see what happened to people when they encountered her son. It did not seem to matter whether they were shepherd or king, man or woman, priest or prophet: when they looked on him with humility and let the word of God work in them, their countenances were changed; they were lit up from within.

Another nobleman stood to his feet. Now Mary could see how tall and broad-shouldered he was, his powerful physique accentuated by the billowing crimson robe falling in loose folds from his shoulders. She gazed up at him timidly, a little peasant girl in a homespun dress. She glanced uncertainly at Joseph. What should she do? Should she offer these rather overwhelming visitors refreshment? She had nothing to offer! But before she could voice her concern, the large man spoke reassuringly through the steward's interpretation: 'Please don't be alarmed. It is him [indicating Jesus] we have come to seek, and him we have found!'

He gave orders and soon two perspiring men struggled in with the handsome carved chest that Joseph had seen earlier. They placed it in front of Mary and opened it. She was startled to see that it contained treasures of gold – ornaments, plates and goblets, and a few bags of gold coins. The large nobleman in the crimson robe bowed and explained, 'This is my offering: gold for the infant King.'

Mary and Joseph were speechless, but before they could recover themselves and try to stammer out some thanks, another servant brought in an exquisitely carved box. Melchior stepped forward and removed the lid. The heavy smell of frankincense stole out and hung in the air. Quietly and humbly he put it down by the chest, saying, 'I offer this in worship, as I would in the temple of a deity, to the one I recognise as sent from God.'

Behind him stood another man holding an alabaster vase of extraordinary beauty, so fine and delicate as to be almost translucent. The grey-headed astronomer removed the stopper and soon the heady fragrance of liquid myrrh mingled with the incense.

Myrrh! Mary shivered. The dizzying perfume assailed her senses and brought a sudden foreboding to her heart. The only time she had smelled myrrh before was when a rich man in Nazareth had died and her mother had helped prepare his body for burial. They had wrapped him in grave-clothes impregnated with myrrh and the strong scent had clung to her for days. Suddenly Simeon's prophecy came vividly to mind: 'A sword shall pierce your heart.'

The large majestic astronomer in the crimson cloak, whom the others addressed as Caspar, explained via the steward that they would now return to the inn. Then tomorrow they must go back to Jerusalem and seek audience with King Herod.

Herod! Joseph was startled. Why had this not occurred to him earlier? Of course, influential emissaries from other countries must pay a respectful visit to the Judean king!

The steward realised he had left out a vital piece of the story. 'We went there first, of course. As my masters were seeking a new king they naturally expected to find him in the royal apartments in Jerusalem. But King Herod, though polite and hospitable, seemed much surprised by our quest. Nevertheless, he called in his counsellors and they consulted together and came up with a prophecy that a Messiah would be born in Bethlehem. When we discovered that Bethlehem was only a few miles away, we decided to leave immediately, although it was already afternoon. Then as dusk fell, the star appeared more bright than ever! We were overjoyed. King Herod made us promise to report back to him if we found the young king so that he too could come and pay homage. So we intend to seek audience with him tomorrow.'

Mary and Joseph looked at each other, excited and disturbed. Ever since the angel Gabriel had visited Mary, she and Joseph had had to get used to meeting a strange assortment of people – angels, shepherds, prophets, foreign astronomers. Must they now expect a visit from King Herod himself?

She looked down at the child curled up in her arms. His eyelids were drooping sleepily and he yawned. She caressed him and he snuggled closer. She was conscious of a fierce desire to protect him from any more prying eyes. He was her baby. But when she looked up again and saw the shining faces of those wise men; when she thought of the distances they had travelled so far from home, and their joy when they saw Jesus, and their humility as they bowed the knee and poured out their wealth, she knew that although Jesus was flesh of her flesh she could not possess him, own him, isolate him. He did not belong to her alone.

The astronomers took their leave respectfully and clattered off into the night with their entourage. The star had sunk below the crest of the small hill, yet its glow was still sufficient to light their way back to the inn. Mary and Joseph stood and watched the retinue wind its way down the street, then went back inside.

Once again the house was a quiet pool of serenity. The extraordinary visit seemed dreamlike and unreal; yet there on the floor lay the magnificent carved chest with its golden treasure, the box of frankincense and the exquisite flask of myrrh. Quietly, Joseph stowed the incense and myrrh into the chest along with the gold. Then he pushed it against the wall and covered it with a blanket. The carvings on it intrigued him. He looked forward to examining it more carefully by daylight tomorrow.

He turned and watched Mary as she gently washed the baby and settled him for the night in the little crib that he had made. She glanced up and found Joseph looking at her with serious eyes. He came and put his arms around her and drew her to the bed. A great wave of inadequacy engulfed him. He sighed. 'Will it always be like this?' he said tiredly. He pointed to the chest on the floor. 'What on earth are we going to do with that?' he asked. 'Who knows what will happen next!'

'Joseph!' Mary tugged at his sleeve. 'Do you think King Herod really wants to come and see Jesus? I wouldn't know what to say! He's a great man – but untrustworthy. What shall we do?'

Joseph blew out the light and held her close. Whatever happened, their trust was in God. Mary remembered her response to Gabriel: 'I am the Lord's handmaid; let it be as you have said.' Not only was Jesus not hers to possess, she herself was no longer her own.

7

Down to Egypt

Matthew 2:13–23

Joseph stared uneasily into the darkness. Something had changed tonight. The coming of these wealthy, influential, aristocratic men from Eastern provinces had somehow lifted their lives into a new dimension. They were not just an anonymous young couple with a baby boy. He and Mary were known about in high places. Joseph did not want to enter the world of intrigue and politics. Not for the first time he struggled with the situation he found himself in. Why him? Why Mary? The responsibility was crushing. Suppose he failed? Suppose Jesus was hurt? Or kidnapped?

He turned over. 'I'm a carpenter. I make yokes. I don't want to carry burdens – I didn't ask to. This is bigger than I can bear!' In his crib, Jesus made a small sound in his sleep. Joseph slid out of the bed and crept over to the crib. Small sucking noises reassured him that the little boy had found his thumb. He hung over the crib and listened. 'I love this boy!' he thought.

He lay down again and closed his eyes. Soon he slept. In his dreams he saw again the impressive figures of the wise men. They were bowing respectfully, but this time before a man with a foxy, shifty-eyed face. He sat upon a throne and wore a crown. As the foreign astronomers talked, he nodded solemnly as if in agreement. But somehow Joseph could see that he wore a mask. When his guests had left the room, he tore off the mask and revealed a face of savage cunning. Then, as happens in dreams, Joseph was in the streets of Bethlehem. Figures were fleeing in terror, little children screaming, and hoof-beats of gigantic horses were thundering through the houses, and all the while the shrill hysterical wailing of grief-stricken women filled the air. Joseph sat up gasping, sweat pouring off him, his heart pounding.

Mary reached out, 'Joseph, Joseph! Hush! You're dreaming, my love. It's all right. Go back to sleep.'

Joseph lay down again, the vivid images imprinted on his mind. How could he sleep? Yet he did, and dreamed again. This time a glow of light filled the room and a man stood before him. Joseph had seen him before and waited humbly. Clearly, urgently, the man spoke: 'Joseph! Take Mary and the young child and leave immediately for Egypt! Stay there until I tell you to leave. Herod is going to search for the child to kill him.'

In an instant Joseph was wide awake. There was no one there, but a faint glow lingered in the room. He had received instructions, but he was calm and clear-headed. There was no time for panic; he simply had to get up and get on with the job.

He shook Mary and whispered urgently. 'Mary! Wake up! We have to leave. Now!'

Sleepily she asked, 'Why? Where are we going?'

'Egypt,' was the brief reply.

'Egypt! That's funny!' She smiled and turned over.

'Mary! Wake up!'

'Oh, Joseph, I'm so tired. Can't we go in the morning?'

'No, there's no time to lose!'

'You don't really mean Egypt, do you? Why Egypt? Why now? We can't just go in the middle of the night. I've got to pack.'

Joseph had lit an oil lamp and was already dressing. He came back to her and patiently recounted the dreams he had had.

'It was the same person who came to me before, when I was so perplexed after you told me you were pregnant. I think it must be the angel Gabriel who came to you.'

Mary sat up, alert now, and swung her legs over the side of the bed.

'God has spoken to you, Joseph. He has warned us. Let's go!' Her first thought now was for her little son. Disturbed by the light, he awoke and began to whimper. 'Darling, don't cry!' she said, picking him up and hugging him. 'Daddy is taking us for a ride. Mummy will give you a drink in a minute.' She soothed him and put him down again, then quickly packed their few clothes in a large leather bag. Joseph was outside harnessing the donkey to the small cart he used for transporting the implements and furniture to sell. Now he began to pile his tools into it, working as quickly and quietly as possible. The starlight was still strong enough to see by.

Mary gathered her few pots and pans and put them in the cart. Then she and Joseph heaved up the wooden chest left by the wise men a few hours ago. There was just enough room to add the little crib. Fortunately they had not accumulated many possessions during their short stay in the rented house.

Thoughtfully, Joseph left a few gold coins from the chest for their landlord to find as payment. Then, casting a last look over the place they had called home, they shut the door and left as dawn began to break.

It was a long weary journey to Egypt. They were grateful for the gold coins from the chest as they made it possible to buy food and stay at inns along the way. They reached Hebron after a long day's hard walking with barely a break, stopped for the night and pushed on again early the next day. It was hard-going over the barren rocky hills of the Judean desert, but Joseph thought their chances of being pursued and overtaken would be less this way than if they took the more populous coastal route.

By the time they reached Beersheba, they were very tired and Joseph felt they had put enough distance between themselves and Jerusalem to stay and rest for a couple of days. Many travellers coming up from the Negev stopped at this ancient city to water camels, sell merchandise, exchange news and generally refresh themselves. After the glaring sun and endless vistas of sand and rock, it was delightful to rest one's eyes on green vegetation and to exchange the lukewarm and stale liquid from the bottom of a skin bottle for water that was clear and cold.

As they were leaving the hospitable inn on the third day, they were hailed by a familiar figure coming through the gateway. It was the steward of the distinguished astronomers. He bowed and greeted them elaborately, expressing surprise at seeing them so far south. Mary and Joseph explained that they had been warned of danger in a dream and had decided to leave immediately for Egypt.

At this the steward's eyes widened in astonishment. 'You may remember that we had intended to return via Jerusalem and report back to King Herod. But that night in Bethlehem my Lord Melchior had a very vivid dream in which he saw Herod seeking out the young child Jesus to destroy him. A shining being – he thought it was an angel – urged us not to go to Jerusalem at all, but to return using an entirely different route.' He threw up his hands and rolled his eyes. 'So here we are, making a detour to the coast, where we thought we might pick up a few things from traders – spices and oils and whatnot – and then we have to decide whether to continue north along the coast or go east through Aram and Edom.'

He grimaced and laughed. 'Whichever way we choose it will be months before we see the fair land of Persia again.' Then his dark face grew sombre and his eyes lingered on the little boy on Joseph's shoulder. 'There is some distressing news,' he sighed. 'You did not leave a moment too soon. A couple of days after you left, soldiers on horseback ransacked Bethlehem. We heard they were looking for children under two years old.'

Mary and Joseph listened in horror as he told a grim tale of little children being slaughtered. He turned his head and spat in disgust. 'What kind of a king is that who is so unsure of his throne that he resorts to wholesale murder of innocent children to secure it?' Realising too late that his somewhat insensitive delivery of the news had caused great distress to this young mother, he tried to retrieve the situation. Clumsily he put out a hand and patted Jesus. 'Hey, little fellow, you're looking good!' He turned to Mary. 'He's a handsome boy. I'm so glad he's safe. Well, look after him! May all your travels be in peace and safety!'

Joseph courteously asked him to convey greetings to his masters, and they parted, the steward to his party to find their way back to Arabia, and Mary and Joseph to continue south to Egypt.

Mary recalled that long journey south: the physical discomforts were far outweighed by the heartache she felt at the news of the tragic events in Bethlehem. She felt as if a knife had been thrust into her heart and twisted. If Joseph had dismissed the dream, if they had delayed their going by as much as a couple of days, they themselves would be childless by now! But although Mary was thankful beyond words for their escape, her heart was wrenched with pain for those bereaved mothers; and to add to her pain was the confusing awareness that somehow it had been precipitated by the presence of Jesus. She began to perceive something of the fulfilment of Simeon's words, that Jesus would be the cause of the fall and the rise of many; and especially that a sword would pierce her heart. Again the sense smote her that she and Joseph had been caught up in something immensely beyond their ability to control. That Jesus' coming would be good news was one thing; but that it would stir up such frenzied forces of hatred and brutality she had been unprepared for.

For a long time the little party journeyed on, talking little. Mary and Joseph were wrapped in sorrow and perplexed that their little boy should be the intended focus of such savagery. They did not allow themselves much rest for fear that Herod's soldiers might even now be pursuing them. So they journeyed on, praying for protection as they retraced the ancient paths of their ancestors down into Egypt.

Many years went by before Mary began to understand the symbolism of that journey. For although they came from the house and lineage of David, their ancestry went way back beyond to Abraham, Isaac and Jacob, as did all Israel's. The first Joseph had been sold into slavery and taken to Egypt. Eventually he had risen to become the most influential man in the land, and his family migrated there to avoid famine. There they found shelter and provision and multiplied to become a numerous nation. The Pharaoh became threatened by their growing numbers, so subjugated and enslaved them.

So Egypt became synonymous with slavery and oppression. For 430 years Israel suffered in cruel bondage until a mighty deliverer, Moses, arose to bring them out. Under him, Israel was freed from slavery and received its identity as a nation. It also received the Law which structured the people's worship and way of life.

Perhaps it was necessary that the Redeemer should walk where Israel had walked; to go down into Egypt, the place of oppression, and be brought up out of it again. It was a fore-shadowing of what would one day take place: the going down into the bondage of death and coming forth out of it victoriously, the first-born of a new race who would follow him and receive his law written on their hearts.

But Mary did not yet comprehend all this as they came towards the Nile and saw the pyramids rising from the sand on the horizon.

So they fled from their native land to escape cruel oppression, as countless families have done through the centuries. Jesus was no stranger to the homeless and victimised. He himself lived as a refugee in an alien land during the early years of his humanity.

Then Joseph, his human guardian and protector, received further instructions in another dream and the family travelled northwards again, eventually to take up residence in Nazareth in Galilee. Thus Matthew, who would join Luke in recording events and who alone would tell of the eastern astronomers' visit, could apply the prophecy of Hosea to him: 'Out of Egypt I called my son.'

8

Virgin Birth?

*Acts 1:1; 9:1–19; 19:9; 28:11–16, 30–31;
Romans 3:23; 5:1–12; 6:16–23; 1 Corinthians
1:26–31; Galatians 4:4; Ephesians 2:1–8*

It was a warm day in Rome. In his villa on the north side of
the city, Theophilus was sitting in his shady courtyard under
a vine, reading a manuscript. Here on the hillside at least a
breeze stirred the leaves above him, whereas down in the city
by the Tiber the atmosphere was sticky and fetid.

He put the manuscript down and called the slave to bring
another glass of wine. He had almost reached the end of the
scroll, and felt strangely moved by his Greek friend's account
of this man Jesus. Staring out over the city, with its
columned temples, the Coliseum, its many marble statues
and elegant villas, his mind wandered to the small Jewish
province of Galilee. He had been there once, when he had
visited the garrison at Caesarea. He remembered the lake
nestling like a jewel in the folds of the surrounding hills, and
the little fishing communities dotted around it. This was the
area where the subject of Luke's narrative had spent most of
his life. It all seemed so small and distant.

But it was in Ephesus that he had met Luke. He had fallen
sick with a fever and had needed a physician, and someone
had found Luke and brought him to his bedside. He had

been impressed with this cultured Greek who had travelled widely around the Mediterranean. He was also impressed with his skill and his caring manner. Luke made regular visits to his patient, and Theophilus, bored and weak during his convalescence, looked forward to them.

He could not remember exactly when it was, but at some point he had asked Luke curiously what was the secret of his peaceful demeanour; it contrasted so strongly with the turbulent lives of others around him, and indeed with his own stressed lifestyle.

Luke's reply had startled him. Instead of talking about diet or a regime of daily baths or the merits of some potion, he had begun to talk about an inner peace he had got from someone called Jesus. On subsequent visits, Luke told him more about Jesus. He came from that obscure and troublesome little province of Galilee – a good man, but seemingly unjustly treated, and eventually suffering death by crucifixion.

Theophilus shrugged and grimaced. Most unpleasant! But not uncommon. Sometimes, especially in these out-of-the-way provinces, Rome had to resort to rough and ready methods to quell riots and keep order. But Luke went on to say that that was not the end. Apparently the man had come back from the dead! Theophilus was intrigued, but not convinced. However, as Luke went on to explain the significance of these events and how they had affected his own life since he realised this Jesus was the only Son of God, Theophilus became increasingly interested.

Luke's friends also worshipped Jesus and in fact held meetings to teach about him in a hall not far from where Theophilus was stationed at the time. The leading speaker was a man called Paul, who was particularly well known for his passionate oratory about this Jesus. When he was well enough Theophilus went to hear Paul speak in the Hall of Tyrannus. Paul was not particularly impressive looking –

short and swarthy with a hooked nose – but there was an intensity, an energy about him that made his lecture the most electrifying thing that Theophilus had ever heard.

'He almost persuaded me to be a Christian!' he thought. He was recalled to Rome soon after, so he had not heard Paul again. But he had seen Luke once more and had extracted from him a promise that he would set out for him in orderly fashion the life of Jesus of Nazareth so that he could study it at his leisure.

And now the scroll had arrived and had been with him day and night as he eagerly devoured its contents. He knew by now that he could not simply dismiss Jesus called the Christ from his mind. But he had many questions and longed to find someone who could help him understand.

When his steward was bringing him up to date in the office the next day, he was amazed to hear that Luke's friend, Paul of Tarsus, was here in Rome. He had been brought in chains all the way from Caesarea for allegedly provoking a riot in Jerusalem. Theophilus knew that the Christians in Rome were most unpopular at this time. Years earlier, Caesar Augustus had started the cult of emperor worship, so worship of anyone else, except the accepted deities, was interpreted as treason and regarded as a threat. This was perpetuated by ensuing Caesars who began to use Jews, and then Christians even more, as scapegoats on which to pin blame for any calamity.

So he knew it would be imprudent to advertise his interest in the Christian faith. He could end up isolated, ruined, imprisoned – or, worse, in a dark alley with a dagger in his back. He needed a discreet way to visit Paul without provoking too much comment. He walked home thoughtfully.

Great was his joy when he entered his villa to find a visitor waiting for him. Sitting on the terrace enjoying the view of Rome in the setting sun was Luke! Exclaiming with joy, he heartily welcomed him, and soon Luke was telling him how he had landed at Ostia, the port of Rome, two weeks ago, after an extremely hazardous journey lasting several months. He had come with Paul, to support and be of service to him in any way he could during his imprisonment. 'You will get an account of our travels in due course,' he said, explaining that he was now engaged in the sequel to his first book.

Theophilus was pleased to discover that Paul was not held in some stinking dungeon, but was under house arrest in a small rented house near the Forum. It should not be too difficult to see him after all, especially as he could go as an official escort to the physician. They spent a pleasant evening together before Luke went back to his lodgings in the city.

Theophilus made a few discreet enquiries and eventually acquired a special permit to gain access to Paul. So a few days later he and Luke met in the Forum and made their way together to the small square house.

It was heavily guarded. Theophilus showed his permit and after some wrangling, during which some silver coins exchanged hands, they were allowed in. They went to a room upstairs; a guard was posted outside.

Paul was sitting by a table near a window with rolls of parchment and quills scattered around untidily. When Luke entered he rose with unfeigned joy to embrace his dear friend and colleague. Eventually Theophilus was introduced and was soon talking about Luke's narrative of Jesus which he had been reading so eagerly.

Paul rubbed his hand through his thinning black hair and smiled ruefully. 'Ah, Luke!' he exclaimed. 'How much I need your writing skills! My eyesight grows worse and sometimes my hand gets stiff and shaky. See what large scrawly letters I write! I need your neat fast handwriting. I am full of thoughts I need to set down and write to the churches.'

Then he turned courteously to the Roman. 'Am I to understand that since you have read Luke's manuscript with some enjoyment your presence here is not just in an official capacity?'

Theophilus nodded. 'I have been able to procure a special permit for Luke to come in and out freely as your personal physician and supply your needs. As his sponsor, I am glad of the opportunity to talk with you personally. I heard you giving a lecture in Ephesus at the Hall of Tyrannus once, and ever since then I haven't been able to shake off the idea that Christianity is more than just another religion. Now I have read Luke's excellent work.' He stopped and looked helplessly at the Jew and the Greek. 'What is it about Jesus that fascinates me so?'

Eagerly, Paul and Luke both started talking at once, then stopped and laughed. 'Let's start at the beginning, like Luke did in his writing,' suggested Paul. 'We need to establish who Jesus is. The whole thing began in God's heart. He sent his Son to become a man, born to a virgin . . .'

Theophilus interrupted him. 'But that's my first question! Why a virgin? Is it important? And was she really? A virgin, I mean. You have to admit, that takes some believing. Why could he not be born to any woman?'

Paul turned to Luke. 'You tell him,' he said. 'Was Mary just "any woman"?'

Luke was not to be rushed. Characteristically careful, he answered thoughtfully and exasperatingly, 'Well – yes and no.' As Theophilus frowned uncomprehendingly, he went on, 'You know I promised to investigate everything thoroughly. Wherever I could I interviewed eyewitnesses of all the events in Jesus' life. I managed to find Jesus' mother, Mary, and talk to her. I wish I could have had longer. We had so little time and I had so many questions. But the things I recorded were just as she related them to me. I wanted to record history with accuracy. So, leaving aside the theological significance for the moment, Theophilus, I have the mother's word from her own lips that when the angel came and told her that she would bear the Christ child, that though betrothed, she was a virgin. In fact, if you remember, she questioned Gabriel, saying, "How can this be, since I am a virgin?"'

Paul interjected, 'You didn't answer my question, Luke. Was she just "any woman", or was she special in some way?'

Luke had a faraway look in his eyes as he recalled the little elderly woman he had talked to in the sunset of that soft Galilean evening. Special, or ordinary? You could pass her in a crowd and never notice her. When the angel had first come to her she was a little peasant girl in her teens, looking forward to getting married. She had done nothing that could mark her out as being particularly deserving of the honour of mothering the Messiah. In fact when the angel hailed her as 'highly favoured' and 'blessed', she had been puzzled, even fearful, as to what that could mean.

Slowly, after a reflective pause, Luke said, 'She was an ordinary person, a young girl in a small town in an obscure corner of a small nation under Roman power. Of course, I met her when she was quite old, but my guess is that she may have been pretty when young, but not necessarily outstandingly attractive. At that stage in her life, she had not had time to develop great depths of character or accumulate much knowledge. There probably wasn't anything very special about her,' he ended apologetically.

'So what you are implying,' Theophilus interjected, 'is that God could have chosen anyone to carry his Son; that the initiative was all his; I mean, she had done nothing to qualify her for this honour.'

Paul heartily approved of this speech. 'Exactly! In fact, what often appears so important to us in terms of human qualifications, such as noble birth, wealth, knowledge, or physical strength or beauty, doesn't interest God at all. Quite the opposite. He deliberately chooses people whom the world considers foolish in order to shame those who think they are wise; and those who are despised in order to bring to nothing what the world considers important. This is so that no one can boast about their own achievements in the presence of God.'

'Let's get this straight,' Theophilus said, digesting this and attempting to get back to the virgin birth. 'All right, Mary was an ordinary young woman, but amazingly, a virgin, who found she was going to be pregnant. Should I care? I mean, why should that affect what I think about Jesus?'

'Wait a minute,' pleaded Luke. 'I said "yes and no" when you asked me if Mary was special. I wouldn't want you to think that she was a total nonentity. Far from it. I believe she was a very special person. I wish you could have met her. There was a sweetness about her, a gentleness that was so winsome. But there was also a sense of dignity and strength. But I happen to think that it was what happened to her and the response she made to God that lifted her out of the ordinary. Before the angel came and told her that God had a plan in which she had a vital part to play, she was nobody important. What I am trying to say, Theophilus, is that God did not choose her because she was special, but his decision to put his life within her made her special. She had a unique calling.'

Paul became excited. 'This is the nature of the grace of God!' he exclaimed. 'He chooses people who have nothing to commend them. In fact we are so hopeless that we are as good as dead. But rebellious and disobedient though we are, because of his great mercy he calls us out of darkness into light, forgives us freely and puts his Spirit in us to empower us to do the works he has planned for us. . . .' He paused for breath and Luke took advantage to bring the conversation back.

'Paul is right. Mary had a unique calling; but so do we all. We discover it when we respond to God. We also have a destiny – to be holy and blameless – and we can only fulfil that call by being empowered as she was. Think about what happened next,' he went on. 'She asked a question, "How will this happen, since I am a virgin?"'

Theophilus nodded. Luke continued, 'The angel said, "The Holy Spirit will come on you." Do you see? This is a supernatural event. Something – Someone – holy was going to come down from heaven. Jesus was not conceived in the ordinary way. He is God, yet clothed in flesh.'

Paul was quick to refine this point. 'Not just "clothed in flesh"; he actually became flesh. His humanity was complete. He truly was man,' he insisted. 'But you see, my friend, he had to be a perfect man – a sinless, spotless man.'

'Why?' asked Theophilus.

'It all goes back to the very first man, who was called Adam. He was spotless in the beginning. But unfortunately he did not stay that way. He disobeyed God's specific instructions. When Adam sinned, sin entered the entire human race. Adam's sin brought death; so death spread to everyone, because everyone sinned.'

'Everyone?'

'Everyone. There is no difference. Everyone has sinned and come short of God's holy standard. So because everyone is tainted by impurity, even our good acts are not good enough to raise us up and make us worthy of heaven. There is a fatal flaw in us all, even the very best of us.'

Theophilus leaned forward, his eyes sombre. 'So really what you are saying is that there is no hope for *anyone*. If we all carry this . . .this . . . seed of rottenness within, then we are without hope.' He twisted his hands, looking down at the floor. 'I know I'm not perfect!'

'And yet a holy God cannot accept less than perfect: that

would be to deny his very essence,' Luke chimed in. 'We are not perfect, and can never make ourselves perfect, so we truly are without hope unless there is someone who is qualified to help us. That Someone has to come from heaven, because all human life is sinful; but in order to rescue sinful man, he has to be a man. It could not be an angel.'

'That's right,' affirmed Paul. 'One man made everything go wrong by his disobedience, but by one man's act of obedience everything can be made right.'

'Hold on,' said Theophilus. 'Presumably this man is Jesus of Nazareth. But why is his obedience so different from everyone else's?'

Paul's face was alight. 'Because of who he is!' he declared. 'Because there is no one like him, or ever will be!' He sprang to his feet, unable to stay still because of the overpowering emotion as he thought about the glorious man who had waylaid him on the Damascus road, and turned his life upside down and become his friend. After a quick turn around the room he came and stood in front of the troubled Roman.

'Oh, Theophilus! Oh that you might know him! I was so different from Mary. I was not humble and gentle. I thought I was someone important. I was the most upright Jew that ever was, a Hebrew of the Hebrews. I hated the Christians because I thought they were liars and blasphemers. I was a proud and rigid Pharisee. Then one day – I was on my way to Damascus to hunt out some Christians and throw them into jail! – a blinding light shone from heaven. I fell off my horse and heard a voice saying, "Saul, Saul, why are you persecuting me?" Do you know, it was Jesus. I had thought he was some fraudster who had been tried and executed, rightly so in my view, and was dead. But here he was – alive! All that he had claimed about himself was true. And he told me he had chosen me – *me!* – to be a bearer of his life!'

He paused for breath and Luke was quick to add, 'As you can see, my friend, we know and love Jesus, but I realise we haven't yet explained why he is uniquely qualified to help us in our hopeless condition. The heart of it is that God deeply loves the human race, and his desire has always been for us to share his glory. Then sin brought an impenetrable barrier between us and him.'

At this point, Paul realised they needed to clarify to the Roman how sin had entered the picture. 'There is a third party, you see, Theophilus. God has an enemy, Satan, who is implacably against him and the objects of his love. This enemy, the devil, knew that if he could entice men to rebel, they would be in his power, robbed of their friendship with God and their inheritance with him in glory. He would be the supreme ruler on the earth. So his plan was to tempt Adam and Eve, his wife, to disobey. They were originally created to have authority, to rule in the earth. But when Adam chose to obey Satan, he became Satan's slave. Mankind truly is in bondage.'

A great seriousness had entered the room. Paul continued: 'So a way had to be found to redeem fallen man and recover his lost authority and cancel the effects of sin. God cannot just wink at sin; it has to be paid for. The only way to defeat the devil was for a man to come and do what the first man Adam had failed to do – live a pure life, untouched by sin, and then die the death that all men deserve to die. That way any legal claim the enemy might have on mankind would be broken.'

Light was beginning to dawn in Theophilus' under-standing. 'I see. The only one who could pay the price to buy us back had to be a human being. So he had to be born into the human race through a human womb and live a human life. . . .'

'That's right!' interrupted Paul. 'But no son of Adam

could qualify because they were all slaves of sin. A member of the human race had to be found upon whom Satan had no claim. It looked hopeless, but God found a way. In the fullness of time, God sent his Son, born of a woman. Since Jesus was conceived by the Holy Spirit he was not a fallen son of Adam, and therefore Satan had no claim on him. If Jesus had been the ordinary son of Mary and Joseph (or anyone else for that matter), he would have been Adam's descendant and therefore Satan's slave.'

'What an amazing plan!' murmured Theophilus. 'I think I'm getting hold of it now. We were helpless to help ourselves. Only God could help us. But he could not wave sin aside. So we needed someone who was not a slave to sin – someone who was morally perfect, which only God can be; yet a man, to do what Adam did not do: live a sinless life, and then die to pay the price for our wrongdoing.'

He stood up and paced to the window where he stood looking out over the Roman Forum mellow in the light of the setting sun. Paul and Luke glanced at each other, aware that this was not a moment on which to intrude with talk, but to retire into the background and let the Holy Spirit work. They sat quietly until darkness fell and the soldier outside brought in lighted candles.

Theophilus turned round blinking in the candlelight and faced the two men. 'Why?' he asked. 'Why would he do that? He didn't have to leave heaven, be born in a stable, live a clean life, never do a thing wrong and *die*. What did he gain?' Yet as he looked at the glowing faces of the two friends, Jew and Greek, he knew the answer.

'Us!' shouted Paul.

'You?' queried Luke.

Theophilus closed his eyes. The love of God overwhelmed him. 'Me,' he said.

9

At Home in Nazareth

*Luke 2:39–40; 2 Corinthians 5:16–17; Hebrews
2:14–15; 4:15; 5:8–9; 7:26*

Nazareth. An obscure village in a disregarded valley in a
despised province in a conquered land. 'Can anything good
come out of Nazareth?' Such was its reputation that no one
expected anything remarkable to be associated with it.

One spring morning a bearded man led a donkey and cart
up the track from the plain of Jezreel. By his side walked a
woman in her twenties and in front skipped a lively little boy,
clothed in a simple homespun tunic. The grass around was
bright with the flowers of spring and the air was soft and
warm. Mary and Joseph looked about them with the
contentment of homecoming travellers after a long absence,
enjoying the familiar landmarks, so ordinary and yet so precious after long exile. Here was the well, and here the first
small white houses on the edge of the town. Gardens were
scattered among them, bordered with hedges of cactus in
which grew fig trees and olives, and the air was fragrant with
orange blossom.

Now they passed through the market-place, which was
bustling with activity. Mounds of fruit and vegetables were
heaped colourfully, bales of cloth displayed, bowls of spices
jostling for attention with locally made pottery, trinkets and

ornaments, and carved implements, and of course people milling about looking, examining, bartering, buying. Joseph picked his way through with the donkey, and Mary called Jesus to her side and held his hand tightly. He looked around with bright, curious eyes. This was Nazareth, his home town which his mother had told him about!

They came to the narrow street that wound up from the market-place. Here was the olive tree, outside the carpenter's shop, under which Mary spoke of her pregnancy to Joseph, and where the angel spoke to him in a dream – a place of poignant memories for them both. Jesus looked up at Mary as Joseph put his arm around her and they smiled at each other, remembering.

And now here was the shop itself, and the door was open. But before they could go in, someone was running down the street shouting and laughing, quickly followed by others and suddenly they were swallowed up in a welcoming, smiling, hugging group of relatives and friends. Willing hands took the bridle of the donkey and helped pull the cart. Someone hoisted Jesus onto his shoulders and they all surged up the path to the home of Mary's parents where a welcome home feast was being prepared.

Mary's mother's arms went round her daughter, holding her close. The two women clung to each other, speechless for a few moments. What can be said to bridge the gap of several years? All words suddenly seemed trite and inane. Mary gazed at her mother's face; there were more lines than she remembered, and the once black hair was now pre-dominantely grey.

The mother looked searchingly at her daughter and saw a mature poised young woman in her prime. There was a serenity and joy shining out of her that brought peace to the mother's heart and a smile to her lips. Unspoken fears were laid to rest. Mary was well and happy! She looked forward to some confidential chats. She wanted to know all about their travels, where they had lived and what their homes were like. She wanted to know how the marriage was progressing (though she wouldn't ask directly, of course, just watch and observe and perhaps drop a few discreet leading questions) and especially how she had coped with the birth of her baby. But all in good time! First she must get acquainted with her grandson.

She relinquished Mary at last and turned to look for the little boy. He was sitting on a bench by the wall with his grandfather, gazing up at him solemnly with a finger in his mouth. The old man was talking softly to him, playing some little game. His hand circled over the child's head and swooped down to tickle his tummy. The boy broke into delighted laughter, wriggling and squirming.

Mary's mother could not take her eyes off him. 'Oh, Mary! What a beautiful child!' she breathed ecstatically and hurried over to hug and caress him.

Home! Mary sighed contentedly. A place to be loved, accepted, to belong. A place to be cushioned against life's knocks, to be comforted and cared for, a refuge, a shelter. But a place also of nurture, development and training, to be made ready to take one's place in the world with confidence and yet humility.

She watched her parents who had so faithfully loved and cared for her from babyhood to marriage, now engrossed with her son. A deep desire flooded her to mother this boy well, to do everything in her power to facilitate his mission in life. What a huge responsibility was hers! 'I want to build a good home!' she silently told herself.

So what was the home in Nazareth like? It was the dwelling of a carpenter of a provincial village, and therefore not lavish, but not achingly impoverished either. It was simple and modest, the home of a man who worked hard with his hands to fashion ploughs and yokes and other implements. A few mats or carpets were scattered around and the bedding, rolled-up quilts, was stored by day on a shelf or in a recess, and unrolled at night. Earthenware vessels for daily use were ranged around the walls on ledges, and a few items of furniture were placed here and there – a table, some stools, a chest, a cupboard. At the door stood the large water-jars of red clay which had to be refilled every evening.

The food which Mary served was simple and wholesome: rice and meat, then stewed fruits. After the meal the youngest member of the family would pour water over each person's hands from a brass jug into a large basin.

Mary was glad that after the events surrounding Jesus' birth and the fugitive years in Egypt, they could live a plain, uneventful life in the seclusion of this small town. Herod was dead. Mary could spin and cook and go to market and visit the well with her pitcher on her shoulder without fear of murderous pursuers. Jesus played and learned and helped his parents in their daily tasks, and went with them to the synagogue on the Sabbath.

So he learned the experience of being a human son, raised by human parents. Joseph and Mary, mindful of the teaching in the Book of Proverbs – 'Train up a child in the way he should go' – were zealous to make sure that he knew the Scriptures. Every Jewish boy learned to recite the Shema from an early age: 'Hear, O Israel! The Lord our God is one. You shall love the Lord your God with all your heart, with all your soul, and with all your strength,' and the collection of Psalms known as the Hallel, the Songs of Ascent. His knowledge of the Law and the prophets became deep and extensive.

When he was about five, he was old enough to go to school. Each day, except on the Sabbath, Mary watched him run down the street to join his friends on their way to the school in the synagogue. His everyday language was Aramaic, but he understood Greek as well, since it was currently spoken in some of the surrounding towns such as Caesarea and Tiberias. Hebrew was not a language commonly spoken, but he was taught to read the Talmud and recite the Torah in Hebrew at the synagogue school; and he also acquired a smattering of Latin, since the Romans were in occupation and were influencing the culture with their architecture, games and laws.

Mary watched her son grow up; he was well-liked, as well as unusually wise for a young boy. One by one, brothers and sisters were added to the family, so to his human experience was added that of brotherhood. Like any mother she was aware of the undercurrents, the ebbs and flows in the relationships, the atmosphere, the moods and feelings of different individuals. She quietly observed their interaction with one another, glad when all was harmonious, and sad when, as every mother has to from time to time, she had to intervene in squabbles and arguments. But this was not very often, because Jesus had a happy, peaceful effect on the home and was a good example to the other children.

She was thinking about it all one day, many years later, in John's house where she had lived since the crucifixion. The persistent and attentive Luke was at her side, pen poised over parchment, gathering material for his book. They had reached the part where the family had come back to Nazareth.

'But what was he really like?' he insisted, his doctor's mind hungry for detail, and his natural curiosity getting the better of him. 'What did he look like? Was he good-looking? Did he ever get sick? How did he get on with his brothers?'

Mary smiled. 'Every mother thinks her son is beautiful. I was no exception. It's difficult to see him through other people's eyes, but yes, *I* think he was good-looking. And strong. Working with Joseph made sure of that!'

She remembered him trotting alongside his earthly father to the workshop even as a little boy of four or five. First Joseph taught him to help tidy the room, sweeping up the wood chips and hanging the tools neatly on hooks on the wall. As he grew bigger, he could shift planks and he learned to use the saws and to split logs with the axes. He developed carpentry skills by watching his father and copying him.

'I remember looking at his hands one day when he was about eleven,' she told Luke. 'They were strong and well-shaped, the fingers long and supple. He was good at making things, even at an early age . . . very creative.' She caught his eye and they both laughed, suddenly conscious of the absurdity of this innocent remark.

'But earlier than that,' she went on, 'when he was still a little boy, he came home one night and after supper he fetched the broom from its place behind the door and swept the crumbs off the floor. I looked at Joseph. He was watching him with satisfaction. "I taught him to sweep the workshop today," he said. "Now he knows it is something he can do to help." Jesus finished the job and went outside to dispose of the crumbs. Then Joseph turned to me and said, "He is so teachable! He absorbs everything I say. He is quick to learn, and once he gets hold of what I'm telling him, I don't have to tell him again. He's a joy to have around!"'

She recalled the wonder in his voice. Then he had pointed at Jesus' little brother, James, who was mischievously prodding the new baby, Jude, who was falling asleep. 'Now James here, he's a different story! You can tell him to do something till you're blue in the face, but if he doesn't want to do it, he won't!' He laughed, but was quick to add, 'But I love them both!'

Mary felt the same way. She loved all her sons and daughters, but Jesus *was* different. He loved his brothers and sisters and they loved him and looked up to him, not only because he was the eldest, but because he was everything they could want in an elder brother. Not only was he caring and loyal, he was a good companion, fun to be with, quick-thinking and a vivid and witty story-teller. He was also undeviatingly honest and would not join in anything hurtful or underhand, and that sometimes presented problems.

Mary recalled an illuminating incident. One day little James was naughtily gathering wood chips behind a low wall, and hurling them over at the house next door. Every so often he managed to get one through the open window. A cry of vexation would be heard, followed by the emergence of the lady of the house, looking cross and puzzled. Meanwhile James was hidden behind the wall, shaking with laughter. Jesus found him engaged in this enjoyable pursuit, and restrained the giggling child, explaining that this was not kind or helpful to their neighbour.

James glared at Jesus, annoyed, and ran in to tell his mother that Jesus had spoiled his fun, and he had meant no harm, he was only playing!

'Jesus was right, you know,' she gently admonished him.

'I know!' bawled the sulky child. 'But why is he always right? Why can't he sometimes be wrong?'

It was a question that Mary found difficult to answer. It was true – Jesus *was* always right. She was reluctant to embark on explanations, partly because she herself only dimly understood, partly because she was sure that the children would not understand, and partly because she was unwilling to imply that he was more loved or favoured than they were.

The fact that he was always right mostly made life easier. His rightness was not a sort of self-conscious, self-exalting, arrogant superiority. She did not have to coax him to be good like she did the other children, or bribe him with sweets to behave better, or punish him for disobedience. Neither did she have to reward him for an extra-special effort, because all his efforts were excellent. He was just . . . good. There was a shining purity about him that was compellingly attractive.

And yet it was also uncomfortable to live with sometimes because it exposed everyone else's crookedness. People liked the strong, tall, open-faced boy, but sometimes they feared another sort of strength – the refusal to compromise, a total commitment to speak the truth and the courage to take an unpopular stand. His thoughtfulness for others and respectful attitude, as well as his happy disposition, won him many friends. But alongside him some people felt inadequate and dirty, and they hated him. Rather than face their need to change, they tried to drag him down to their level in order to make them feel better about themselves.

To his friends he was an enigma. It appeared he did not even *want* to do some of those things that they found so deliciously tempting but knew they ought not to indulge in, and this they found irritating.

Mary, watching his friendships and interactions with his classmates, saw a subtle game gradually develop. 'Let's try and get Jesus to do something bad today!' Many times she would hear a scuffle going on in the street outside. With a sinking heart she would run outside in time to see a band of tormentors running off, leaving Jesus picking himself up from the dust. She knew it was another attempt to get him to abandon his self-control, lose his temper, and lash out in fury. Her heart ached, and ached still more when he came in bruised, his eye black and his lip cut, to stand silent before her, refusing to lay blame or give in to self-pity or anger while she washed off the blood and dirt. She never heard him utter the words, 'It's not fair!'

At those times, Mary struggled with a mixture of emo-

tions. Part of her cried out in indignation. She longed to
protect him, to defend him, to urge him to use those muscu-
lar arms to put up a fight. To stand by and watch this unpro-
voked bullying was hard to bear. The sword was piercing her
heart again. And yet she saw something else emerging out of
these encounters: the formation of a godly character, a submission to a higher authority, and a steadfast, focused
commitment to a life not motivated by selfishness. Then the
urge to encourage him to lay hold of his destiny would over-
take her protective mother's heart, and tears of frustration
would turn into tears of love and amazement.

'Sometimes,' she told Luke, 'when some nasty little thing
had happened that was designed to smear his reputation and
wear him down, I would lay my hands on his shoulders and
say, "Go for it, Jesus! Keep running the race! God is with
you, my darling son." I can see him now, looking up at me
with those great big shining eyes. He would say things that I
didn't really understand at the time; things like, "My Father's
will is the most important thing to me." Those kinds of
things became clearer in his teaching years, but I can see now
how he was learning obedience to the Father in the things he
suffered even then.'

She stood up and shook out her dress and moved over to
the doorway. Leaning on the doorpost she gazed out at the
rocky Ephesian landscape behind John's home, but in her
mind she was seeing the Galilean hills above Capernaum.
She told Luke, 'That's where he taught the people, "Love
your enemies, do good to them that hate you, pray for them
that are spiteful to you." That was not just theory to him. He
had learned it from boyhood up.'

This reminded her of another incident. 'He lost his cloak
one time. It was winter and very cold. I must confess, I was
annoyed because it was new, but I knew he would not have
been deliberately careless, because he wasn't like that.

Anyway, he discovered that it had been taken by another boy who had been quite hostile to him, who came from a poor home. Jesus went down to his house – to get it back I thought – but he returned later without it. Then I discovered he had given the boy his tunic too!' She sighed and shook her head. 'What could I do? I couldn't tell him not to be generous!'

She came and sat down again. 'So you see, Luke, it was not always straightforward raising him. I found that often my assumptions about what was right and wrong had to be adjusted. He seemed to have another way of seeing things.' She struggled to explain to the fascinated Luke. 'He was never disobedient to me or Joseph. In fact he modelled obedience to the other children. They were motivated by his example and, I hope, love and respect for us! But for them it was always a struggle and they couldn't keep it up. But a higher allegiance kept him faithful; I think it was this devotion to the will of God.'

Mary realised that she had not even referred to the pivotal part of his life. How did he know the will of God? She began to tell Luke how Jesus quickly discovered the track behind their home which led up to the top of the hill on which Nazareth was built. When he was very young, she used to take him there and they would explore together. These were some of her happiest memories, when they wandered hand-in-hand, watching the eagles fly, picking the flowers, and listening to the harsh cry of the ravens. Jesus would chatter away happily by her side and she taught him the names of the flowers, and songs and rhymes. Then as more children came along, they would become family occasions, with picnics and games. But one day, when she went to wake him, Jesus was not in his bed. He had got up early and climbed the hill to have time alone to pray.

'How old was he?' Luke wanted to know.

Mary was vague. 'Oh, I don't know. Ten maybe, or eleven.

But when I knew where he was and what he was doing, I stopped worrying about it. I think he began to realise who he was quite early on and learned to listen to God whom he began to refer to as "my Father".'

She stopped. It was getting cool and Luke rose to shut the door. He lit the oil lamp and turned to look at Mary. She was an old lady now, and time and suffering had left their marks on her face. He felt a rush of love and gratitude that she had submitted herself to the will of God those many years ago – not only to lend her womb to bring forth the Son of God, but to commit herself to nurture and shelter him through his growing years. Her eyes were shut and he was about to leave quietly when they opened again. 'Are you tired?' he enquired gently. 'Shall we leave it for today?'

'Remind me to tell you tomorrow about what happened when he was twelve,' she said. 'You must not leave out that bit of the story!'

Intrigued, Luke assumed that this had something to do with his adolescence.

Mary told him to wait and see, but his words had triggered her memory again. Now in her mind's eye she could see the group of teenagers in the village. Jesus grew, like all the other boys, through the normal stages of puberty. Suddenly it seemed they were little boys no longer. Their voices deepened and hair appeared on their chests and chins. The little girls turned into pretty young women with graceful figures and alluring smiles. How did Jesus cope with the explosion of hormones fizzing through his bloodstream?

'I watched him make choices. The young maidens would come down the street past our house looking for him. I think he presented something of a challenge! But he just smiled. Sometimes I would hold my breath when a pretty girl came into the workshop, outwardly demure but with invitation written all over her. But he always behaved with courteous friendliness and never gave a hint of preference for any of them. You know, he often had to make choices that resulted in misunderstanding and loneliness.'

'But he did it. He kept going. He didn't sin!' Luke exclaimed. 'Surely it was in these secluded years that a great part of his work was done. He must have fought and won many battles that prepared him for his public ministry and were training for the ultimate victory of his death and resurrection.'

Mary looked at him searchingly. 'You are right. And I think they should be kept secluded.'

Luke was taken aback. 'But think of it! A sinless childhood, sinless boyhood, sinless youth, sinless manhood – spent in humility, ordinary daily work, submission, contentment, prayer, obscurity. What an example!'

'Yes, obscurity,' Mary repeated. 'Perhaps it should remain that way. How can you ever convey the complexity of the development of a man who was also God? Will it not give rise to much unnecessary speculation? I think it important that you make known his conception and the manner of his birth. But after that, perhaps you should concentrate on the three public years. It is enough to know that he shared in our humanity that by his death he might destroy the devil who holds the power of death.'

Luke was silent. It was true. He would have the utmost difficulty in conveying this complex material. He remembered something Paul had taught in Corinth: 'Though we once regarded Christ [from a worldly point of view], we do so no longer. Therefore, if anyone is in Christ, he is a new creation; the old has gone, the new has come!' Most people who followed Jesus now and in years to come, would most probably also be ordinary men and women living their lives in obscurity. All that was vital to sustain their life in Christ was embodied in his incarnation and three years of ministry, death and resurrection. It was enough to know that because he identified with them, having suffered and been tempted, he is able to help those who are also being tempted.

Luke took up his quill and wrote simply, 'They returned to Galilee to their own town of Nazareth. And the child grew and became strong; he was filled with wisdom, and the grace of God was upon him.'

IO

Anxious Parents

Mark 9:33–37; Luke 2:41–52; Psalms 122; 123; 125; 126

'Have you seen Jesus?' Mary tugged at Joseph's elbow.

He turned from the conversation he was engaged in with a couple of friends, and looked at her anxious face. 'Jesus? Don't worry, Mary. I'm sure he is with his friends. When I saw him last he was with Joel and Nathan.'

'But that was this morning!' fretted Mary. 'I don't think I've seen him all day!'

Joseph frowned. 'I did tell him yesterday that now he is twelve he need not travel with us all the time, and he could walk with the other boys. He is probably among them.' He could see that Mary was not convinced, and good-naturedly offered to find him, sure that she was worrying unnecessarily.

Mary went back uneasily to the hastily erected tent where the rest of her brood was settling down for the night. This was the first upsetting incident during a Passover feast that up to now had been unmarked by any accident or problem.

Every year Joseph and Mary went up to Jerusalem for the Passover with a crowd of pilgrims from Nazareth. The children spent most of their lives in Nazareth, hardly ever going as far as the next village, so this was a real adventure. They had helped load up the cart enthusiastically, with rolls of bedding, water bottles, loaves of bread, some fruit, cooking utensils, flour and oil, as well as extra clothes, especially blankets and cloaks. Jerusalem was perched up amid high hills and could get quite cold at night. They also took along tent poles and coverings to make a tent to bed down in at the stopping points along the way.

Some people brought lambs with them which they had carefully bred and reared for the Passover sacrifice. Others would wait to purchase a lamb from the Temple precincts, secure in the knowledge that it would pass the priests' examination for any disqualifying blemish.

It was a happy holiday occasion. Emerging from the circle of hills that surrounded their own little town, the caravan of pilgrims descended to the great plain of Jezreel, where they joined vast crowds of Galileans making the eighty-mile journey south. Through the beautiful spring countryside they travelled, mostly walking at an easy pace, but many women and small children rode on carts piled high with their possessions or on donkeys or mules. The mood was happy and relaxed as families and friends talked and laughed and joked together, enjoying the break from routine, and for those who had done it many times before there was also the savour of nostalgia and familiarity. Stories were exchanged of things that had happened in previous years, of vital items they had forgotten to pack, children's mishaps, and unusual weather, but with the good-natured humour that results from doing pleasurable things together.

The journey took several days and encampments were made at various stopping points each night. Excited children helped erect the 'succoths', or booths, in which to spend the night and were eventually persuaded to settle down to eat and sleep. But as the long columns of pilgrims drew nearer Jerusalem, the excitement mounted. On the fourth or fifth day they began to ascend the steep hills surrounding the city itself.

As the walls and gates and towers came into view, an awesome sound arose. From the multitudes thronging up to Zion came the sound of singing as with deep fervour they sang the Songs of Ascent, the very psalms that King David decreed should be sung as he brought the Ark of the Covenant back to Jerusalem.

The soaring voices, the beautiful solemn melodies and the profound words always brought a lump to Mary's throat. What must it have been like those centuries ago, when King David was so transported with joy that before the eyes of all Israel he had abandoned his outer tunic along with his dignity and danced and sung with all his might? How she identified as she sang with all her heart:

'I rejoiced with those who said to me,
"Let us go to the house of the Lord!"
Our feet are standing in your gates, O Jerusalem!'

But now one of these psalms held special meaning for her:

'Unto you I lift up my eyes
O you who dwell in the heavens.
Behold, as the eyes of servants look to the hand of their master,
As the eyes of a maid to the hand of her mistress,
So our eyes look to the hand of our God
Until he has mercy on us.'

Was she not very specifically the 'handmaid of the Lord'? And had she not, like the maid in the psalm, trustfully acquiesced to his will, believing in his mercy?

She looked across at Jesus walking so purposefully at Joseph's side, and her heart was filled with a rush of deep affection for him. 'My boy!' she thought. 'How good God has been to us!' She looked around her at her other children and at Joseph; then up at the massive walls looming ahead surrounding the city, a fortress, unshakable, beautiful in its strength and situation. The voices of the crowd were lifted up in another psalm:

> 'Those who trust in the Lord are like Mount Zion,
> Which cannot be moved but abides for ever.
> As the mountains surround Jerusalem
> so the Lord surrounds his people
> From this time forth.
> For the sceptre of wickedness shall not rest
> On the land of the righteous . . .'

Suddenly she was jolted back to remembering the angel's exact words about the promised Son: 'The Lord God will give him the throne of his father David and he will reign over the house of Jacob for ever. . . .'

Somehow, this boy of hers was destined to take up the sceptre of righteousness and sit on the throne of a mighty kingdom even as great David had done. What was God's promise to David? The prophet Nathan had declared over him, 'The Lord says that he will make you a house. I will set up your seed after you, and I will establish his kingdom. He shall build a house for my name, I shall establish his kingdom for ever. I will be his Father and he shall be my Son.'

Every Jewish boy knew it and was taught that one day this promise would be fulfilled in the Messiah who would come to sweep away their enemies and usher in a new kingdom.

When she thought of such themes, Mary invariably felt out of her depth. She was tossed to and fro. The enormity, the glory of it on one hand caused her heart to cry out, 'Oh, yes! Let it be as you say!' and yet the sheer unlikelihood, the absurdity that it could ever have anything to do with her ordinary little life in the back streets of Nazareth sometimes caused her to shake her head in doubt. But now, as she made her way up to Zion that bright April day, the word of God ringing in her ears stirred her afresh. In fact these days she was finding that her faith was renewed by two things: looking at Jesus, and remembering what God had said.

Once again she looked at her son. He was a fact, a person, the tangible proof that God had not forgotten his people or his promises. He was the reason why all this was happening.

How much did he comprehend? She had told him, of course, about his birth and what the angelic messenger had said. He was certainly demonstrating that he was an unusual boy in many wonderful ways. But he was also so happily and unpretentiously normal, without any apparent inclinations to grandeur, that sometimes she wondered if he felt any sense of destiny at all.

Now, as they came to the last part of the steep ascent, the voices around rose to a crescendo:

'When the Lord brought back the captives to Zion,
we were like men who dreamed.
Our mouths were filled with laughter,
our tongues with songs of joy.'

The children liked this one. It had a catchy tune and they sang lustily, even the two-year-old clapping his hands and jiggling about on the cart. She suddenly noticed on Jesus' face an unfathomable expression of shining joy and dawning wonder. Around her the crowds were jostling, singing, carts trundling along, lambs and sheep bleating, but he walked as if waking out of a dream.

She watched him approach the gate of the City of David, the sword twisting in her heart again. He seemed so young and vulnerable, yet at the same time there was a nobility, a dawning awareness of what this was all about. The song continued:

'Those who sow in tears will reap with songs of joy.'

'I think,' she said to herself, 'that I have many more tears to shed yet, but I will also believe to reap in joy.' Jesus turned and smiled at her, and somehow she knew that he was anticipating the same things.

The rest of the Passover celebrations took place uneventfully. The lambs were offered, slain and eaten, the questions asked, history recounted and the Scriptures read. As Joseph faithfully taught his family the origins of the feast and as they participated in its ceremonies day by day, Mary noticed a particularly intense interest in Jesus' eyes.

The men and boys were required to attend the Temple only for the first two days of the feast. After that they were free to go home. So because they had a long journey to make with young children, Mary and Joseph decided to avail themselves of this opportunity to leave at midday on the third day.

And now, at this stopping point on the first evening, all this was going through Mary's troubled mind. She was sure they had told Jesus when they were going. She and Joseph had discussed it together and agreed that he could walk back with some of his friends, but that they were all going at the same time. Distractedly she hushed the other children and wandered around the tent picking up discarded clothes and folding them neatly, trying to piece the sequence of events together in her mind. She had just about convinced herself that he was with his friends and that because they were dawdling along they were later than everyone else, when at last Joseph came in.

'Have you found him?' she asked anxiously.

Reluctantly he shook his head. 'No, but I found Joel and

Nathan. They were surprised. They thought he was with us and that we were not going until tomorrow.'

They stood and looked at each other, the full horror of the situation sinking in. They had lost him! Mary wrung her hands. 'What can we do?' she wailed. 'Are you sure you looked everywhere you can think of? Oh, Joseph!'

'Mary, sit down. Let's go through it all again. You're sure that he knew we were planning to go at lunchtime?'

'Well, I think so. Didn't you tell him?'

'No, I was loading the cart. I thought you told him!'

'Joseph! He must still be in Jerusalem! All by himself! Unless . . . suppose he started out . . . suppose he followed the wrong group. He could be in a caravan on his way to Egypt by now!'

Like any other typical mother, Mary was imagining the wildest scenarios. He could be kidnapped, wounded, lost, bewildered, worse. She could not bear it. They must go now!

'Where?' said the more practical Joseph. 'Look, Mary, we must try to be logical about this. There are several possibilities. One is that he is even now nearly here with a group of latecomers; another is that he may have got in with some others who have taken a slightly different route. But I think the most likely is that he is still in Jerusalem, failing to realise we have left already.'

Mary was all for starting back there and then. But Joseph reminded her that they could not simply abandon the other children. They would wait until the morning and he would ask Mary's mother to help her look after the younger children while he went back.

But Mary would not be left behind. So at first light, after a miserable sleepless night, they started back the way they had come, leaving Mary's mother to continue the journey with help from friends.

*

Anyone who has lost a child even for a short time knows the anguish of uncertainty, the torturing fears fed by tragic stories of abduction and death. Added to that is the sense of guilt for supposed carelessness, and feelings of failure as a parent, compounded by merciless 'if onlys'. 'If only we had made sure . . . if only we had double-checked . . . if only I had known . . . done something different. . . .'

But the truth is that even the best parents are not infallible. Misunderstandings arise, mistakes are made and things go wrong because we live in a fallen world. We make wrong assumptions, draw wrong conclusions, relay faulty information and act in ignorance. We cannot provide for every eventuality, although we may do our best to anticipate every possible scenario. A mother's instinct is to protect her children from every danger, but there is always one she has not thought of. And when her child becomes a victim, whether of someone else's vicious behaviour, or of one of life's accidents, unless she is able to receive healing she will flog herself unmercifully and carry the burden indefinitely, recognising it was her responsibility to shield and shelter that child. Either that or she will seek to bury the pain, blank it out – unless of course her torture ends because the child is found well.

Mary was one of us. She was not floating above life on some ethereal cloud, untouched by the difficulties of raising children. Her heart by now was lacerated with the sword of pain and fear. Every mother has a responsibility before God for her children, but how much more awesome must the responsibility have been in caring for the Son of God!

They hurried back as fast as they could, stopping only now and then when they recognised someone they knew, to ask if they had seen Jesus. It was late afternoon when they arrived and now they had not laid eyes on him for a day and a half.

They began to search systematically through all the various encampments around the edge of the city. They kept it up until nightfall, but without success. Even then they patrolled up and down, visiting camp-fires, asking questions and giving descriptions of the missing boy.

The next day they began in the city itself. It was not easy because the streets were thronged with far more people than usual, and choked with temporary shops and stalls. They kept going with a dogged persistence, not daring to admit it was hopeless, not daring to stop. To keep going was to say there was some hope; to stop was unthinkable.

Towards the end of the third day, Mary was emotionally drained. Joseph, looking haggard himself, put his arm around his exhausted wife and insisted they stop and have something to eat and drink. They found a place selling food and sat down. Mary was surprised at how hungry she was. When they had eaten, Joseph said, 'There is only one place left where we haven't searched. That's the Temple.'

Mary perked up. 'Why didn't we think of that before? Let's go immediately.'

Joseph drained his cup and stood up. 'Come on then.'

They threaded their way up through the narrow streets to the Temple area.

On Sabbaths and feast days, rabbis would sit in the cloisters with groups of disciples, engaging in discussions of the Scriptures. Joseph was a pious man and conversant with the Scriptures, but this kind of debate was out of his league. So it was with some trepidation that he and Mary, humble village folk, and despised Galileans at that, ventured into these halls of learning.

They had expected to find little knots of people gathered here and there around different rabbis, but the court seemed strangely empty, until they noticed that a lot of activity was concentrated at one end. They hurried towards it. As they drew nearer their footsteps seemed embarrassingly loud in the intense silence; only one other noise could be heard: the one Mary had been longing for and feared she would never hear again. Several rabbis in their fringed robes were seated on the marble benches that ran around the edge of the cloister and other students of the Law were seated at their feet. In the midst of them, also sitting on the floor, was Jesus. His clear young voice, not yet broken, echoing around the soaring marble columns, could be heard respectfully asking a question. The murmur of a mature voice could be heard in reply, evidently ending with another question. For as Mary and Joseph hurried up, they were astounded to hear Jesus calmly and confidently, though with due reverence, giving a fluent answer.

A gasp of amazement rippled around, and Joseph heard someone nearby say quietly, 'I never thought of that!' But then, before he could restrain her, Mary threw caution to the wind and burst through the circle. Another gasp went round, this time of surprise at her interruption.

'Jesus! Son! How could you do this to us? We've been at our wits' end looking for you!'

Now that the search was finally over and Jesus was apparently unharmed, anger overcame her worries. She was furious! She wanted to shake him! He should know what they had been through, what anxiety he had caused them.

There was an understanding and slightly amused buzz among the debating group. It broke up and the people drifted off in twos and threes. Jesus came towards her and embraced her tightly. She clung on to him and gave him a little shake. 'We were frantic! Your father and I looked everywhere for you!' A tear slid down her cheek and angrily she brushed it away.

He stood back and looked deep into her eyes. 'Why would you need to search?' he said quietly and without apology.

'You should know that the most important thing for me is my Father's business; so you would find me in his house.' As she continued to look into his face the anger died out of her. She did not understand how anything could be more important than his safety; and he had always been such a good boy! What was happening? She looked searchingly at him, frowning slightly. What did he mean, his 'Father's house' and his 'Father's business'? Was it somehow connected to those prophecies about the Messiah?

She sighed, puzzled, tired, but very relieved. She was so thankful to have him back that she just held his hand tightly as they walked through the Temple court and out into the light of the setting sun.

It was strange, but suddenly he seemed more mature and grown-up than she did. He seemed to be talking about a different realm of which she had no grasp and little experience. He seemed to evaluate things with a different measure, to make decisions from a different base of judgement.

She realised now that he had gone beyond her and Joseph's power to control him; he moved to a different tune, a higher command. On this Passover trip he had crossed an invisible line.

They returned to Nazareth and settled back into the ordinary routine of home life. Jesus now applied himself in earnest to learning the carpentry trade from Joseph and was a submissive and willing apprentice. But when he spoke the words 'my Father' now, they knew that he was not referring to Joseph.

In many ways, as mothers do, she mourned for his childhood, now passed for ever. He had reached the age of perceived manhood. Soon he celebrated his 'bar mitzvah' and officially entered responsible adulthood. But although she remembered his soft round babyhood with nostalgic tenderness, she watched his rapid growth into tall young manhood with pride and pleasure, and rejoiced in his remarkably quick mind. Now that she had seen him in action in the Temple among the rabbis, she was more aware than ever how unusually able and wise he was.

However, he had not become cocky, arrogant and distant. He was still obedient and humble and loving to them both. Sometimes, as she watched him absorbed in carving and shaping a yoke or a stool, or giving her a hand with fetching the heavy buckets of water from the well, or good-naturedly joking with his brothers and sisters, she pondered his words. Was this 'his Father's business'? It was puzzling, because if it was, then a lot of 'his Father's business' was carried out in everyday life, not just in the religious moments.

Many years later, when Jesus was finally recognised as the great leader, she was in her sister's home in Capernaum and she heard James and John arguing about who should be the top man. Through the open door she watched while Jesus went over to a group of children playing contentedly a few yards away in the sand with some stones. He came back hand in hand with one little tot to where the disciples were gathered in the shade of a tree. He brought the child into the middle of the group and sat down.

Curious, she strained to listen. Over the sounds of the seagulls and the lapping waters of the lake, his clear voice carried: 'I tell you the truth, unless you become like little children, like this one here, you won't even see the kingdom of heaven, much less occupy a position in it.'

She smiled to herself. His words were not empty. He knew exactly what it was like to be a little child – unpretentious, humble, simply trusting and trustfully obedient. She had witnessed his growing years and she knew his early dependence on his human father. That had been the training ground for his dependence on his heavenly Father. Now, looking back, she wondered if that incident when he was twelve marked the transference of his primary allegiance from human authority to heavenly.

But who could tell? Perhaps he had always known his identity, and that knowledge had been latent within him, awaiting the right moment in his development to unfold and flower into clearer definition.

That had been the point when she realised she could not cling to him as her boy. That day in the Temple she had mentally let him go so that his allegiance to his heavenly Father could be fully worked out for the benefit of all mankind.

He was known as Jesus the son of Mary, but he knew and she knew that he was Christ the Son of God. John, the evangelist, who later became to her as her own son, put it succinctly: 'The Word became human and lived here on earth among us. He was full of unfailing love and truth. And we have seen his glory, the glory of the only Son of the Father.'

11

The Wedding at Cana

John 2:1–12

Amos put down the heavy pitcher with a sigh of relief. That was the last one. Filling the huge water jars at the entrance of the wedding chamber was an arduous business. Thank goodness he would not have to do it again for at least twenty-four hours! There were six of them ranged along the wall of the gallery around the covered courtyard where the wedding feast would be held. Each held about twenty gallons. Usually two of the jars were ample for the daily household needs, and it was his responsibility to make sure that they were regularly refilled. But because of the wedding his mistress had hired four extra ones. Fortunately she had also hired extra servants too!

Preparations had consumed them for weeks now. The head steward had been engrossed in calculating the amount of food and wine that would be needed, working on menus and borrowing more plates and cups. The last week had been particularly hectic; the whole house had been cleaned from top to bottom, furniture rearranged and decorations put up. Yesterday and today there was great exertion in the kitchen. Mountains of rice were cooked, along with several lambs and accompanying vegetables. Piles of fruit were artistically arranged in baskets and the smell of freshly baked bread wafted through the house.

The head steward checked his guest list again and Amos took a few moments to lean on the doorpost in the setting sun. In its waning light he could still see the pathway that the wedding party would soon take, bringing the bride from her home to that of the bridegroom. Already along the route little groups of friends and neighbours and curious onlookers were gathering in anticipation of seeing the bride and cheering her on her way. Garlands of flowers and leaves had been hung beside the path near the house and the evening air was heavy with their fragrance.

Some guests had already arrived and were relaxing in the courtyard, chatting in groups and enjoying a drink before the festivities began. Others were waiting along the way and still others would join the joyful procession behind the bride and groom. Among those who had come earlier in the day was a lady whom Amos knew as an occasional visitor. She came from the town of Nazareth ten miles down the road, where she had been the wife of the carpenter, Joseph.

Everyone for miles around had been saddened by his death some ten or twelve years previously. Not only was he a skilled carpenter whose expertise was very much missed, but he was a kind, friendly and genial man whose integrity and decency had earned him many friends and a good reputation. Amos had only been a lad when he heard of his death and his memory of him was dim, but he had an affectionate respect for his widow. He had been serving in the home of this family for a long time now, and knew her as the sister of his mistress, and aunt to today's bridegroom.

Her name was Mary.

She was sitting outside now, having arrived earlier with one of her daughters. Probably some of her sons, who were cousins to the bridegroom, had accompanied him to fetch the bride and bring her back in the wedding procession. Mary had been helping her sister with some last-minute touches, and now, like Amos, was enjoying a few peaceful moments before the festivities began.

'Hello, Amos,' she greeted him pleasantly. 'How have you been coping with all the wedding plans? Has it been very tiring?' Pleased that she remembered his name, he answered that yes, it had been tiring but exciting and they had all been looking forward to this special day with great anticipation. They chatted about this and that for a while and then Mary asked him if he would fetch her a drink of water. He hurried over to one of the huge water jars and dipped in a pitcher and poured some water into a cup. 'I filled these earlier myself,' he said, handing her the cup.

She looked at the six great jars ranged along the wall and gasped in astonishment. 'What, all of them? That must have taken ages!'

He laughed. 'No, I can't claim to have filled them single handed. The mistress has taken on extra help, but it's my responsibility to make sure that together we keep them filled.'

'What else do you have to do?' Mary asked curiously.

'Oh, a bit of everything,' he said, then added importantly, 'But my main job is to be in charge of the wine. I have to make sure that everyone has what they want, but I also have to make sure that the stocks last for the length of the feast.'

'Not an altogether easy task,' Mary murmured thoughtfully, thinking that as the feast would go on for several days it was difficult to predict just how much would be needed, especially as there were always more guests than originally invited.

She laid a hand on Amos' arm. 'Amos – you have included my son, Jesus, among the guests, haven't you? He has been down in Judea, so he may be a bit late.'

'I'm sure we have,' the young man replied comfortingly.

'But I'll just check with the chief steward.' He went indoors and left Mary sitting in the twilight with her thoughts.

She had not seen Jesus for a few weeks, but rumours had reached her ears about some upheaval going on in the Jordan Valley near Jericho that involved both Jesus and her cousin Elizabeth's son, John. People had been flocking out from Jerusalem and surrounding districts to hear John preach. Apparently it was not a comforting message that he brought, but one of uncompromising sternness of the need for repentance. He was also baptising many in the Jordan as a symbol of their need to be washed clean from their sins.

Evidently this provoked the religious leaders to find out what authorisation he had for this activity. 'I am the voice of one crying in the wilderness, "Make straight the way of the Lord,"' he had replied. When Mary heard that, she had sat very still, her heart pounding, recalling the prophecy of John's father, Zechariah. 'And you, child, shall be called the prophet of the Most High, and you will go before him to prepare his way.'

What had happened next was even more startling. The next day, he had seen Jesus coming to him and, pointing him out to the crowd, he had loudly and boldly declared, 'Behold the Lamb of God who takes away the sin of the world!' Then, somewhat puzzlingly, he had baptised Jesus.

She mused that when she had time to talk with Jesus she would ask him why he had asked John to baptise him. She had also heard that something else had happened that was quite remarkable: a dove, or something like one, had alighted on his shoulder and a voice had been heard saying, 'This is my Son.'

Although she had not yet got all the facts straight, one thing was clear to her: Jesus was going public. At last, after thirty long years of obscurity, when only she and Joseph had any idea of his true identity, now it seemed that he was being proclaimed by John as the Christ. He was also attended by disciples who called him 'Rabbi'. Perhaps his hour had come!

Another thought hit her: 'Suppose he turns up here at the wedding with a band of disciples. Will there be enough food and drink?' She arose swiftly with the intention of finding Amos and warning him. But before she could do so there was a shout, 'Ho! The bridegroom is on his way!' The guests all stood to their feet and ran to the entrance where they could see down the hill.

It was now completely dark, but away in the distance a little group of lights could be seen. It was swelled by other lights joining in behind, and so the growing crowd came on up the hill, the path lined with the torches of onlookers and well-wishers. Faintly at first came the sounds of flutes and drums and singing, increasing in volume as the procession drew nearer.

The torchlight fell on happy laughing faces surrounding the bride, radiant in her beautiful wedding garments, her long hair flowing under the bridal veil. As she came into sight murmurs of admiration rose from the watching crowd. She was attended by her bridesmaids, also dressed in festive clothes, carrying torches or lamps held high to light the way. Some in the procession were carrying flowers and myrtle branches. The whole scene was full of colour and music and happy excitement.

The wedding procession arrived at the door of the bridegroom's home. He gazed lovingly into the face of his betrothed and took her hand, leading her into the courtyard that had been covered with an awning and decked out with flowers for the occasion. They stood together under the *chupa*, a special canopy, and there the bridegroom solemnly vowed to care for her, honour, keep and work for her. After the ceremony the marriage was blessed and they ritually washed their hands. Then the marriage supper began!

The bridal pair reclined together at the top of the square arrangement of low tables, and the guests all took their places. Plates of steaming and appetising food were passed around and the servants were kept busy filling up wine goblets, clearing plates and bringing out yet more dishes.

The night wore on, the guests enjoying the food and conversation, catching up with relatives whom they had not seen for a long time, making new acquaintances and generally taking pleasure in being part of such a happy occasion.

Amos and his team were kept busy from the start. Even before the feast began, equipped with basins of water and towels, they had gone round the table washing the feet of each guest. Hands also needed to be ceremonially cleansed – which was quite a meticulous business – and then rinsed from time to time as the courses of the meal progressed. The eating utensils had to be washed too. So there was much coming and going of the servants between the guests and the great stone water jars.

As was to be expected, the feasting continued for several days. From time to time someone broke into song and it was taken up by the rest of the company. There were times of music and dancing, story-telling and jokes; and all the time the wine kept flowing.

Mary had ample time to circulate among her friends and relatives, to exclaim over the budding beauty of a young niece and the astonishing growth of a nephew; to commiserate over the family misfortunes of an old friend, and rejoice with another at the long awaited birth of a grandchild. Everyone was united in their praise of the beauty and virtues of the bride. Certainly she looked radiant throughout, and the bridegroom bore the appearance of a very happy man.

Mary was glad that Jesus had arrived just as the procession was entering the home, so had been present throughout. He had five friends with him, all from Galilee. In fact one,

Nathaniel, came from Cana and was known to the family of the bridegroom. Mary had been a bit apprehensive when Jesus had arrived with several extra people and went to speak to her sister about it. But her sister, so buoyed up by the euphoria of the occasion, and so relieved that everything was going so well, told her not to worry – there was plenty for everyone, and everyone was welcome! So Mary relaxed and enjoyed herself. She was glad to see that Jesus and his friends were excellent company, eating and drinking with evident pleasure and mingling freely and happily.

On the third day, she was watching some of the younger ones, whose energy levels appeared to be unflagging, whirling around in a dance, when she became aware of Amos hovering nearby. 'He looks worried,' she thought, surprised. 'I hope everything is all right!' She noticed him speaking covertly to one of the servants. The servant went off in the direction of the store where the wine was kept. After a few minutes, Mary saw him slip back and whisper something to Amos. Amos' already gloomy countenance now became distinctly horrified. Chancing to look up at that moment, he found Mary's eyes upon him. She beckoned him to her side and said quietly, 'Amos, I can see something is wrong. What is the matter? Is there anything I can do?'

Amos forced a rather crooked smile, desperately trying to keep up some semblance of normality before the other guests. Then he bent down beside her and haltingly told her the shocking truth: 'I fear that . . . er . . . that we have very little wine left. In fact hardly any.'

'How much?'

'We have just broached the last bottle,' he confessed.

This was serious. Mary restrained a gasp and tried to look unconcerned. She got up and went out in a leisurely way so as not to excite comment, her mind busily engaged in possible solutions. Amos followed her and stood abjectly beside her. 'I shall have to tell the steward,' he volunteered resolutely.

'No, not yet,' said Mary quickly. 'Don't do anything that could bring shame on the family!'

'I already have!' Amos objected.

'There must be something we can do,' declared Mary with more confidence than she actually felt. 'Perhaps we can run out and buy some.' She caught sight of Amos' doubtful expression. 'No, too far to go. Anyway, we couldn't get enough for this number of people in time. Oh dear, what are we to do?' She knew that if the dilemma became public, it would place the host family in an extremely embarrassing situation, and cast a blight on the unblemished happiness of this wedding.

Suddenly the solution came to her with shining clarity. Of course! Jesus was here. Surely he would know what to do! After all, he had been publicly proclaimed in Judea by John the baptiser as having greater rank than him, and the one they were all waiting for! Here was a wonderful opportunity for him to disclose himself in Galilee too. She turned brightly to the downcast Amos. 'Don't worry,' she advised decisively. 'I will tell my son, Jesus. He will know what to do!'

Amos stood outside the door near the water jars and watched her slip in and make her way unobtrusively to Jesus. Amos shook his head. 'How could this man Jesus help?' he wondered. 'Did he have a secret supply of wine somewhere?'

Mary reached Jesus, and touched his arm. She had no doubt at all that this problem was well within his scope to deal with. The man conversing with Jesus gave way respectfully when he saw that his attention was claimed by no less a person than his mother. Mary managed to draw Jesus slightly to one side. She looked up into the face of her beloved son, confident that he would do this for her. After all, he was her son, and if he were truly the Son of God, he could easily use his power and get this delightful young couple out of a fix.

Away from the crowd, out of earshot, she took his hands and said to him simply, 'They have no more wine. . .' and smiled, waiting.

Slowly, he dropped her hands and stepped back from her slightly, as if to put a little space between them. 'Woman,' he said gently but firmly, 'why should that concern you and me? Why should I be caught up in your affairs? My time has not yet come.'

Frowningly she looked up at him, perplexed. It was so unexpected. Hurtful even! He had not addressed her as mother – almost as if he were denying his relationship with her. She felt as if she were being rebuked by her son – unthinkable! Unfair! Such thoughts were racing through her mind as she stared at him doubtfully. Should she remonstrate with him, express her indignation, her disappointment? Or . . . it occurred to her, not for the first time, that he never acted unfairly, and he had never given her cause to believe he did not love and respect her. But now as he stood before her she saw not just her son, but a mature man who would not allow their human relationship ever to influence him or manoeuvre him into doing anything that was not in line with what the Father was saying. He would not be pushed into disclosing his true identity as the Son of God, nor would he be manipulated by the mother–son relationship.

She understood. His time of submission to her was over. She had no specific claim on him. He would not act just because she was his mother. But he was still the Son of God – he was still able, he was still trustworthy! And if God wanted him to act, he would. Her tranquillity returned. She drew a deep breath and turned back to the agitated Amos. 'Whatever he says to you, do it,' she instructed.

Afterwards, she reflected that that short sentence was wisdom for life. Things were truly reversed now. It was no longer whatever she said to him he would do; he was not a child. But neither was he a tame magician who could be relied upon to come running whenever she crooked her finger, nor a genie to make life easier whenever she rubbed the lamp. No. He was the Son of God; he would do whatever he had decided to do. And whatever he said to do would be good and right and acceptable.

Amos called his team of servants. They stood in a line before Jesus. 'Take your orders from him,' said Amos briefly. Then he wished he had not, because what Jesus told them to do seemed a waste of time.

'Fill up the water pots,' Jesus told them.

Amos nodded at the bemused servants. 'You heard him – get on with it!'

Hurriedly they grabbed their buckets and went out to the well. They filled them there, returned and emptied them into the huge pots. This took quite a while as the supply had begun to get low. At last the task was done. A perspiring servant poured in the last bucketful and all six jars were full. They stood still, panting, and waited for the next instruction.

It came as quite a shock. 'Now, draw some out and take it to the head steward.'

Mary, watching Amos' face, was amused at his look of total bewilderment. He looked at her beseechingly, as if to say, 'Do I really have to?' She nodded at him: 'Do as he says, Amos.'

Although it was so bizarre, Mary was confident that everything was under control. It was Jesus' responsibility if anything went wrong. She felt quite relaxed. Not so Amos! In total fear and trepidation, he dipped a pitcher into the water and carried it to his exacting overseer. He fully expected that this would be the end of his employment with this family.

The head steward saw him coming. 'Oh, there you are,' he said. 'I've been looking for you. We need more wine. Is that what you have there? Pour me some, would you?' Amos' hand shook as he lifted the pitcher and began to pour. Mary saw him gasp. A tremor went through him as incredulously he watched deep red liquid flowing into the offered goblet. The steward saw nothing amiss and took a deep draught. 'Aah!' he exclaimed appreciatively. 'That's the best wine we've had so far. Hey, Amos! Where have you been hiding this? This is good!'

He went over to the bridegroom, leaving Amos speechless and trembling. 'Taste this!' the steward implored. 'This, you must agree, is the most excellent wine! Most people serve the best wine first, and then when everyone has had plenty and they're a bit less discriminating, they bring out the poor stuff. But we've kept the best until now!'

This was considered a great joke. Everyone laughed and pressed forward to try some. 'Amos! Where did you get this?' someone cried.

Faintly, as in a dream, Amos gestured to the door. 'It's in the water pots,' he croaked. They all laughed, thinking that he had imbibed a bit too freely himself. One of the servants went out with an empty pitcher to the large pots, followed by a boisterous, good-humoured crowd. They watched him dip it in, and then pour out rich, glorious, full-bodied, aromatic wine.

There was total silence. 'It was him! He did it!' said Amos hoarsely, pointing at Jesus. Heads swivelled and people near him stepped back a little, awe and something like fear on their faces.

One of the five men accompanying Jesus was John, who later wrote an eyewitness account of the whole event. He would become very well known to Mary, and when she lived in his home in later years, he often recalled this moment, because it marked a turning point in his life.

'When I saw that miraculous wine I was . . . amazed, stupefied. Someone thrust a cup of it into my hand and I remember just sitting there, staring down into it. It was so incredibly, robustly, richly red! I stared at those great water pots, reminding myself of how carefully I had washed my hands in the prescribed manner and how those pots symbolised something in our traditions and culture; something I had thought unshakeable, unchangeable; a way to approach God, a way to get clean. I wanted to be clean – not just on the outside, but inside. A few days earlier, I had been in Judea and was amazed to hear John the baptiser proclaiming that Jesus was the Lamb of God who removes the sin of the world. This had introduced a whole new way of thinking to me. Was it possible that he held the key to what really pleases God? Was there another way of getting clean – permanently?'

Mary nodded. 'Anyway, you came along to this wedding . . .'

'Yes, I was already feeling in my heart that I must get closer to this man. Then he somehow made wine from the very thing symbolising our purification! Was this also symbolic? If so, what was God saying? I looked around at all those people happily drinking the wine: the bride and groom, the parents, the friends and relations. Such a warm, joyful atmosphere prevailed. Some began to dance again; there was music and laughter.

'Then – I shall never forget – I glanced up at Jesus. He was standing there, looking so delighted. He turned and our eyes met. Suddenly I thought, "No one has ever seen God, but his only Son, who is himself God, has come to make him known." I began to realise that God is not the way I had thought he was; he is different, and Jesus had come to show us what he is really like. Something new was happening – a new day was beginning. . . .'

His voice trailed off. 'Of course, I did not understand then what it was all about. But it was as if a corner of a curtain had been lifted, and I got a glimpse of glory. This man, with a word, had done the impossible. But it wasn't a conjuring trick. It was a sign, and its significance was only just dawning on me.'

As always, when he was giving an account of the story, he was overcome with wonder. 'Oh, Mary! He was the Word; he became flesh and lived among us. We beheld his glory. But that was the first time. I knew then that he was the Christ, and I believed in him.'

Mary remembered it well. She had been in a good position to see John's reaction. She saw him sitting dazed, looking into his wine tumbler, then at the water pots with an intent, thoughtful expression. Then came the moment when he had looked into Jesus' face and been captured for ever. He slid off his seat and knelt on the ground.

After the wedding, Mary and her other sons, James, Jude and Joses, decided to spend a few days with friends and relatives in Capernaum, a busy and prosperous little fishing town on the northern shore of Galilee. Jesus and his disciples went along too, and it became a centre of Jesus' ministry over the next three years.

One evening she was sitting on a rock at the lakeside. The fierce heat of the day had subsided and the tranquil waters reflected the surrounding hills. It was a scene of calm beauty, yet Mary felt a tinge of regret. Evenings like this always reawakened in her a sadness at her loss of Joseph. She thought about the wedding she had just attended and went on to recall that of one of her own daughters. A couple of the boys were married now too.

Someone else was wandering along the beach. As he drew near she saw it was Jesus. He came and sat down beside her. 'What are you thinking about?' he asked.

She looked away at the hills, purple and blue now in the dusk. 'I was thinking about weddings,' she said dreamily, and added hesitantly, 'I suppose I am a little sad that I shall never sit at a wedding feast where you are the bridegroom; at least I don't expect that you will ever marry.'

There was a long pause; she thought he was not going to respond. When he did, it was nearly dark and she could not see his face. But his voice was so full of joy he was almost laughing. 'One day I shall come for my bride,' he said, 'and you shall be there at the marriage supper!' He jumped up and pulled her to her feet. 'And the wine . . . it will be the new wine of heaven!' He whirled her round and shouted rapturously, 'And we shall dance on golden streets!' He threw his head back and flung out his arms, laughing and spinning round and round.

Mary thought it was a nice idea. She was slightly mystified, but smiled, glad to see him happy.

12

Family Matters

Matthew 12:46–50; Mark 3:31–35; Luke 4:13–31; Ephesians 3:14–19

Vigorous sounds were issuing from the carpentry shop. James had taken it over as his particular domain since Jesus had begun moving around the countryside preaching and teaching. Mary was glad. It was comforting to hear the familiar sounds of the hammer and chisel and lathe being used. It reminded her of Joseph and gave her a sense of the continuity of family life. But today it occurred to her that the sounds were a little more energetic than usual. She paused on the way to the well, bucket in hand, and listened, frowning slightly. Hammer crashed on nail in a succession of noisy blows.

She sighed. James wasn't happy! She knew her boys. They all had their different ways of reacting to life's dilemmas; Jude would become argumentative and explosive; and Joses, sensitive like his father, was quiet and reflective; but James' way was to retire gloomily into his own solitary thoughts, distancing himself from the rest, stubbornly gnawing away at a problem. Today he was using a carpentry job as a personal anvil on which to bang out his frustrations.

She understood the reason for his current moodiness. She was not the only one who sometimes found Jesus' words and ways hard to understand and hard to receive without offence. His brothers, James, Jude, Joses and Simon were puzzled by the changes in Jesus' life and inclined to be sceptical of the stories circulating about him.

They had been with him in the same household all their childhood lives, they had eaten at the same table, played with the same friends, been educated at the same synagogue. They played in the same streets, rambled around the same hills. They had washed, dressed and slept in the same room. So it was somewhat surprising to them when people began to refer to him as a rabbi, to speak of him in hushed tones of respect, and follow him around the countryside in droves, hanging on his every word. They knew he had not received special training at any select rabbinic school; he was country born and bred the same as they were.

They knew him! He was just their elder brother – good old Jesus, who fished for minnows with them in the brooks and ponds in the spring, and who used to lie in the long grass with them, watching the clouds sail by overhead while they chewed the succulent grass stems and chatted and joked together. True, he was kind and helpful, always thoughtful of other people, generous and honest; great at making up games, fun, energetic, but – well – he was just, you know, Jesus!

Of course they knew he was a wonderful person and no doubt destined for greatness. Perhaps he would become a really great rabbi like the legendary Hillel or Shammai, and make them all proud of him. He was certainly a deep thinker. He used to come out with some unusual ideas, and he seemed to learn things very quickly and retain them, and he was always ready with an answer to the hardest question.

But really! When you heard some of the things people were saying about him! Crowds were pressing in to hear him speak and there was wild talk about him healing sick people and doing amazing, miraculous things. It was said that he had only to touch a sick person and they would get better immediately.

Now, in the workshop, as he thought about these preposterous claims, James shook his head in disbelief. He had worked in this very room with his brother, and had seen those hands, often! Nothing special about them! Ordinary hands – strong, supple, skilful in the carpentry trade, yes, but healing? Jesus didn't know the first thing about medicine!

James thought back to that embarrassing morning in the synagogue in Nazareth. They had all gone along dutifully as they always did, dressed in their best Sabbath clothes. When they reached the door of the stone building, Mary his mother, his sister, and his own wife had separated from the men and gone to take their places in the women's gallery. Inside, it was cool and dim, the only light filtering in through the high small windows and falling upon the white limestone floor.

At the south end was the movable ark containing the sacred scrolls of the Law and the Prophets. In front of it were the seats of honour for the rulers of the synagogue. James was interested on this particular day to see the chief ruler come over to Jesus. He overheard his murmured request that Jesus should read today's portion from the Prophets. Then the service proceeded in its usual pattern of prayers, passages from the Pentateuch and blessings.

They rambled through it, James only half attending and impatient for the last part, curious to hear what Jesus would have to say, for the reading of the Prophets was normally followed by an address. At last, the Aaronic blessing was pronounced. The *chazzan* or minister for the day approached the Ark and brought out a scroll, unwound the cloths that covered it and handed it to Jesus. Jesus stood at the lectern in the centre and read a portion from Isaiah.

James had to admit he read it very well. It suddenly

seemed so fresh and clear. It was from one of the great Songs of the Suffering Servant: 'The Spirit of the Lord is upon me, because he has anointed me to preach good news. . . .'

Wonderful words! James shut his eyes and listened. Jesus closed the scroll and gave it back to the *chazzan* and sat down, as the custom was, to begin his discourse. James was electrified to hear him say, 'Today this scripture has been fulfilled.' He opened his eyes and sat bolt upright. Whatever did his brother mean? Jesus went on to explain the mission of the promised Messiah. There was rapt attention as the wonderful revelation was unfolded to them.

He seemed to draw to a close. All around James people were leaning forward, or turning to those behind and exclaiming over the teaching. So eloquent! So original! So much more full of substance than usual! 'But isn't he the carpenter? You know, old Joseph's boy? Where did he learn to speak like that?' James himself was bemused. Then he was startled to hear Jesus' voice pick up the discourse again. If only he had left it there! Why did he have to ruin it and embarrass them all? For he went on to say that God was no longer exclusively concerned with Israel, implying that Gentiles could also benefit from relationship with him. Even that he himself was the fulfilment of this scripture, but would not be accepted as such. He would be 'without honour in his own town', but there were others outside the fold of Israel who would receive him.

James was plastered miserably to his seat. How could Jesus be so inflammatory, so incautious? Sounds of anger now erupted. All over the synagogue people stood to their feet, shaking their fists, shouting. Horrified, James watched as a group surged forward and grabbed hold of Jesus and marched him outside. The rest of the congregation quickly followed.

Outside, James looked anxiously for Mary and his sister

and wife. They joined him, their faces shocked and serious.
'What are they going to do to him?' gasped Mary. By now
the mob was some way ahead, pushing Jesus along among
them. It soon became obvious that they were heading for a
steep place and were going to throw him over!

Mary cried out in horror. James began to run, not
knowing what he would do. There were so many of them –
too many for him to challenge. At the same time he was
angry with Jesus. Why did he say all those things? He must
be mad!

He had nearly caught up with them and was panting for
breath, when suddenly a change appeared to come over the
angry mob. They fell back a little, and looked at each other
uncertainly. Jesus stood unharmed in their midst; then he
calmly turned round and walked away. James ran up to him,
ready to pour out his anger and beg him, 'Think of us!
Think of the family! You will have us all in disgrace. How
can you say those things? You must be mad!' But when he
met his brother's eyes, he somehow could not bring himself
to verbalise what he was feeling. Uneasy, he looked away.

He did not see Jesus again for a while. But he heard all
sorts of stories that were circulating around the countryside.
Down in Capernaum, there were reports of hundreds of
people flocking to hear him preach. Demonised people were
reportedly set free, lots of sick folk with all kinds of diseases
were being healed – even the paralysed, even lepers! It
seemed that the whole region was stirred up with his exploits.

James did not know what to think. He was inclined to
think it was all exaggerated and hysterical. But he noticed
that his mother listened eagerly to every report, drinking it
all in, her eyes shining. 'She believes it all,' he thought, a
shade jealously. 'Jesus was always special to her.'

Mary was aware of James' negative attitude and it grieved
her. Like any mother she hated it when her children did not

get along well. She hated any sort of shadow in the family, anything that came between brother and brother or sister. Also, she did not want any of her children to have cause to think that she loved one more than another. But how could she explain that although Jesus was still her son, there was an added dimension to their relationship now? She loved him as her son – oh, how she loved him! – but she loved him also as one vastly superior to her.

If only James would open his mind to admit the possibility that there were some things beyond human reason and knowledge, beyond the surface appearance; that Jesus just might be the one they had waited for! She wished James would at least go and listen to Jesus teaching. She resolved to ask him to take her to see him in action at the first opportunity.

James was also worried about other, more sinister, rumours that were going around. It was whispered in some circles that Jesus was mad or had a demon. Religious leaders were reportedly divided about him. You could either believe him completely; or stand against him as divisive, deluded and blasphemous. James hated the controversy. He hated having people come up to him and ask him his opinion. He did not have an opinion. He wished it would all die down and go away. He wanted a quiet life with a normal brother. Quite frankly, he did not believe Jesus was the Son of God, but he did not want to think him mad either. He was just – Jesus!

One time he heard that Jesus was back in Capernaum, and was so overwhelmed with crowds pressing around that neither he nor his disciples had time to stop and eat. 'Enough is enough!' thought James. 'He is overwrought. He needs help!'

Capernaum was not too far away, about twenty miles, so he decided to go. When he told Mary, she was secretly glad that he had decided to go of his own accord and she hoped that he would hear Jesus for himself and be convinced.

'I'd like to come with you,' she said. In the end, it became a family delegation, with Jude, Joses and Simon coming along as well.

It took most of a day to get to Capernaum from Nazareth. They went up the valley around the northwest side of Mount Tabor and then over the hilly country beyond. Sometime in the afternoon they came to a vantage point looking down over Galilee. They stopped and gazed at the panorama spread out before them, a scene well known to them. But this time they were astonished to see that instead of bare desolate slopes and a limpid blue sea with one or two boats on its surface, the whole area was swarming with people. Streams of them were hurrying down the hillsides, and the surface of the lake was black with boats, all heading in the direction of Capernaum on the north shore. Mary and her sons gasped in surprise.

'Do you suppose they are all going to see Jesus?' one of them asked, amazed.

As they continued on their way they soon discovered that this was indeed the case. There was something of a holiday atmosphere, as families and groups of friends clutching bags of food and extra cloaks, laughing and chatting excitedly, made their way to the little fishing town that could clearly be seen in the distance. All the talk was of Jesus of Nazareth, his wise but revolutionary sayings, and the healings and miracles he had performed.

Mary was deeply moved when she heard some of the stories of those who had been cured, and tears stung her eyes as she watched the blind and the lame being helped along. Once, a cart drew alongside carrying a desperately ill woman. Her body was weak and emaciated, but in her sunken eyes shone hope. There were fathers carrying sick children and tired old men on donkeys. There were beggars clad in rags, and well-dressed women with restless eyes and discontented faces; the strong and the weak.

Mary and her sons soon became part of the needy struggling stream of humanity, indistinguishable, submerged. Inevitably the pace slowed down considerably as all these people reached Capernaum and thronged its streets. They were carried along with the crowd to a small house near the shore which Mary knew to be the home of Simon Bar-Jonas, one of Jesus' twelve disciples. The house appeared to be suffocatingly full of people, while outside the teeming crowds made it impossible for Jesus' family to get anywhere near the entrance.

Mary was full of wonder that so many people believed Jesus could help them. There was a little boy near them with a club foot. How she hoped it would be straightened out! But she was also nervous for Jesus. So many demands on him! Ill people pressing all around him, breathing in his face, clutching at him. No time to rest, no time to eat, the constant clamour of voices demanding this and that. She longed to get him out of there and take him home for a rest. She would cook him wholesome meals, and shield him from curious eyes. She would make sure he slept well and his clothes were washed and mended. If only she could get to him. . . .

She turned pleadingly to James. He was less sympathetic, fascinated that his brother had such a magnetic attraction, but appalled at the swirling sea of clamouring humanity. His ungregarious soul was longing for the quiet solitude of home and he just wanted to rescue Jesus and go. 'This can't be good for him,' he muttered to Mary. 'He must be beside himself. He needs to get a grip on himself, take a break. I'm going to see if I can get in and get him out.'

He disappeared into the mêlée. Mary retired to the edge of

the crowd and sat down under a palm tree with Jude and
Joses, while Simon went to find some water to drink. The
crowd surged forward a little as Jesus appeared at the door
and motioned them all to be quiet. The disciples persuaded
them all to sit down and listen. Then followed one of the
most fascinating hours of Mary's life. The noisy crowd
hushed and became silent, straining to hear every word.

He began with a humorous story, and soon they were all
laughing. Jude and Joses and Simon joined in recalling the
days from their childhood when Jesus kept them entertained
for hours with his stories. But this was not just entertaining;
this story had a punchline that searched out the motives and
secret thoughts of the hearts of his hearers.

Suddenly there was a commotion. A poor man was hauled
through the crowd right in front of Jesus. Jude and Joses half
rose to their feet thinking that this intrusion might be threat-
ening to him, and maybe he would need some help to remove
the man. But it soon became clear that he was blind and
helpless, and could not even speak properly. He stood
abjectly in front of Jesus, making unintelligible sounds.

There was a hush. Mary held her breath. What would her
extraordinary son do now? She could not see his face very
well from this distance, but she thought he seemed to stand
very still. Then in a clear voice, but not shouting, he commanded a demon to come out of the man. Instantly the man
fell to the ground, writhing. He gave one loud shriek and lay
limp and still. Then Jesus got down beside him and touched
his eyes. Into the tense silence came a cry of amazement: 'I
can see!'

Chaos broke loose. People were shouting, gasping. Many
were saying, 'Is he the one? Could Jesus be the Son of David,
the Messiah?' Mary had tears running down her face.

Just then into the uproar strode a party of Pharisees. The
crowd parted respectfully and made a space for them. They

looked around disdainfully and began to make derogatory remarks: 'No wonder he can cast out demons. He gets his power from Satan, the prince of demons.'

Jesus knew what they were saying and called out, 'If Satan is casting out Satan, he is fighting against himself!' The crowd roared its approval. Jesus went on, 'But if I cast out demons by the Spirit of God, then the kingdom of God has come among you!' He went on to teach about demons, and the kingdoms of light and darkness.

Somewhere in the crowd James was sitting. When Jesus had started to teach he had given up fighting his way through the crowd and had sat down. He had watched and listened and been deeply impressed by what had happened. But now Jesus went on to say some very unflattering things about the Pharisees, calling them snakes and vipers. James began to feel very uneasy again. He wished Jesus would not be so uncompromising, so reckless. And was it really necessary to be so provocative? He decided to renew his efforts to get to Jesus and talk to him.

Eventually he found one of the Twelve, Andrew, whom he had met before. They greeted one another, and then James asked, 'Andrew, my mother and brothers are here. We've come to see Jesus, but can't get through the crush. Any chance of you pulling a few strings to get us in? After all, we are his blood relations!'

Andrew put his hand affectionately on James' shoulder. 'Of course, my friend! I'd be glad to help. Let me see what I can do.'

Satisfied that it would not be long now, James went back to the tree where his mother was waiting, and told her he had got a message through. They waited expectantly. James even felt a little sorry for all these people who did not have an inside track. He was lucky to be 'family' and therefore to have some prior claim on Jesus' attention.

He watched Andrew squeezing through the throng to Jesus, who bent his head to hear Andrew's request. He saw Jesus lift up his head. There was an enigmatic expression on his face, James thought. Was it pain? Sadness? Whatever it was, he was totally unprepared for what happened next. Jesus said, 'Who is my mother? Who are my brothers?' Then pointing to his disciples and then to his followers in the crowd, he went on, 'These are my mother and brothers. Anyone who does the will of my Father in heaven is my brother and sister and mother!'

James was devastated. Crushed. Mary laid a hand on his arm, but he shook it off, and walked away down the beach, fuming. The other brothers turned to Mary, troubled. The youngest one, Simon, said falteringly, 'What does he mean? Doesn't he want to see us? Doesn't he love us any more?'

Mary knew she must never apologise for Jesus, never dilute what he said. She longed to reduce the impact of his words, take the sting out of them, but she knew that sometimes, if people were to grasp truth that was so near and yet so foreign to their traditional ways of thinking, it had to shock. It had to come like a bucket of cold water thrown in the face. If it were presented pleasantly, gently and inoffensively, they would never really hear it, and it would lose its power to change.

Eventually they recovered the unhappy James, who remained sullenly unresponsive for several days. They stayed overnight with her relative Alphaeus, and set out the next day for Nazareth. Undeterred by Jesus' strange remark, Mary asked one of Alphaeus' sons, James, to send loving messages to Jesus. She was confident that they would soon meet up with him again.

On the way back, the disappointed brothers discussed Jesus' words. Was Jesus disowning them? Did he not believe family to be important any more? And how could all those people who were not related be 'family'? Did being a brother hold no significance for him?

Mary let them talk. But when they reached the spot with the beautiful view over the lake, they all sat down to rest and have some food, and she tried to help them understand.

'I believe that family is very important to God,' she began. They nodded, agreeing, as any Jew would. 'It was God's idea in the first place. It was his design. It reflects something about God. I think he loves the whole idea of family life, and decided that the best way for us human beings to live is in families.' She recalled a verse from the Psalms – 'He sets the solitary in families' – and said reflectively, 'We need relationship. None of us is self-sufficient.'

'True, Mother,' agreed Jude. 'So we should guard our family relationships. Yet Jesus, who is a teacher about God – in fact, some are saying, is from God – does not appear to appreciate that.'

'Let me tell you something that happened to me,' Mary offered, and went on to describe what Jesus had said to her at the wedding at Cana. 'When I expected him to help because it was I who asked him, he distanced himself from me. He did not address me as mother, and said something like, "Why should I concern myself in your affairs?"'

Four pairs of eyes gazed at her seriously. Jude frowned. 'That sounds quite rude!' he protested.

'Only if you choose to take it that way,' Mary swiftly responded. 'You see, we can choose to be offended, or we can choose to humble ourselves and learn. I heard him say once that he is a rock of offence. You either stumble over him and pick yourself up and carry on, having learned a lesson; or you allow the rock to crush you and lie in the road, telling yourself you are mortally injured, and never move on from that point!'

There was silence as her words sank in. 'I suppose I let

myself be hurt and offended,' Simon said slowly. 'I believed for a moment that he didn't love us any more.' He looked away over the sea. 'I couldn't bear that!' There was a tremor in his voice.

'But I still don't get it!' exclaimed Jude. 'I understand that he was not denying us or deliberately insulting us, and that he wanted us to learn something. But what was it? I'm missing something here!'

Mary took a deep breath. 'It's all to do with who he is,' she explained gently. 'He came into our family from God, because God wanted him to experience family life. But I'm learning that everything he has experienced and participated in is preparation for something much bigger. He truly is your brother, just as I am his mother. But, my dears, he is much bigger than we are! He cannot be confined and fenced in by human relationships any more. He does not belong only to us but to the whole world.'

She looked tenderly at her four sons sitting around her on the grass. 'We are so privileged!' she exclaimed. 'God sent him to us to be the Saviour of the world. We have had him among us in our family for thirty years. We must let him go and do what he has to do, and be who he has to be. You see, he has a much bigger plan in view than just being your brother.'

All this time James had said nothing. He was a peace-loving man and disliked controversy. But he knew now that whether he liked it or not, he was going to have to come to some conclusion about Jesus. He could not keep life safe and tidy, for ever resisting change. He was not ready yet to embrace him wholeheartedly as the Son of God as his mother had done. But his mind was being stretched and enlarged. It was uncomfortable but necessary.

He would have been amazed if he had known that not many years would elapse before he would not only be convinced of the deity of Jesus, but he would boldly and publicly declare him as Saviour in the face of great persecution. But for most of the next three years he remained stubbornly at a distance, yearning secretly for the closeness of brotherhood which had been such an integral and precious part of their growing years; and yet unwilling to share him with the needy, demanding crowds.

James was to be unutterably shocked by the manner of Jesus' death. In spite of the terrible charges of lies and blasphemy that were the apparent reasons for such a violent execution, he knew his brother to be a good man! Profoundly depressed, he characteristically withdrew to the solitude of his workshop. Nothing made sense any more! Why should a good man have to die?

Then came a day that changed him for ever, that turned his melancholy and doubt into joy and belief. Was it up on the hills above Nazareth, or on the shore of Galilee? Maybe it was in the workshop surrounded by tools and woodshavings and sawdust that Jesus met him again and embraced him, forgave him, loved him. It was then that he came to understand; he became a brother of Jesus all over again. Now he was not only related by human ties, but by the blood Jesus shed so that many, including James, might be born again into the family of God.

After that, he gloried in his new family. He had brothers and sisters everywhere, for whoever loved the will of the Father in heaven was his brother and sister and mother also. How glad he was that Jesus had not bowed to the wishes of his human family that day, packed his bag and come home to Nazareth, abandoning his mission and letting family ties dictate.

God loves family. He invented it. The whole concept is infinitely precious to him. It pleases him to see men, women and children dwelling together in harmony, respecting one another, loving one another, complementing one another and deferring to one another. That is exactly how the Trinity of Father, Son and Holy Spirit behaves; and the human family in its small limited way can be a reflection of that glorious heavenly unity.

Jesus knows what it is like to be a brother and a son. He sanctifies those relationships. He related rightly to his human parents and brothers and sisters; he modelled brotherhood and sonhood. But he also demonstrated that the only controlling relationship in his life was between him and his Father God.

God loves family and wants it to be good and strong, not only for its own sake, but because it is intended to be a microcosm of the church, that worldwide network of relationships which is the family of God. James eventually became the leader of the church in Jerusalem and was loved and respected as a 'pillar' among all the early churches. He wrote a letter that was widely circulated among them in which he addressed his fellow Christians affectionately as 'my brothers' or 'my beloved brothers' eleven times! He knew the struggles they were facing as they sought to stand firm under persecution, and he wrote to encourage them. He also pleaded with them to beware of favouritism, to live in harmony and not to be critical and judgemental.

One of his new brothers was the apostle Paul, who described what he prayed might be the experience of every family member – namely, that 'Christ may dwell in your hearts by faith; and that you, being rooted and established in love, may have power *with all the saints* to grasp how wide and long and high and deep is the love of Christ and to know this love which passes knowledge.'

'These are my mother and brothers and sisters . . . those who do the will of God.' Jesus is the firstborn of many brothers.

13

At the Cross

John 18; 19

I shall never forget the sound of the wood thumping and scraping over the cobble-stones, the painful gasps for breath, and the smears and streaks of blood spattering a trail in the narrow street. The people along the way were mocking and jeering raucously, pitilessly; but whenever he drew abreast of them, their laughter fell silent, and all I could hear was that ominous 'thump, thump', and the gasp of agony.

My mind was dull with the horror of it. It seemed unreal. A few days ago he had ridden into the city on a donkey to the sound of cheers and shouts of 'Hosanna!'. Massive crowds had thronged this same street waving palm-branches and had flung their cloaks in the road for the donkey to step on. Such a clamour of joy and expectation! It was like welcoming a conquering hero! 'Surely,' I thought, 'we are on the threshold of a new day! Now that he has been publicly acclaimed, he will soon take a leadership role and begin to govern wisely and kindly like King Solomon. After all, before he was even conceived the angel Gabriel had said that he would have the throne of his father David and reign over the house of Jacob.'

I had been waiting for this to happen all his life, believing that one day he would emerge from obscurity onto the centre stage and take his rightful place as King. As it happens, I was right – that always was the ultimate plan. But I had reckoned without the cross.

I had come up to Jerusalem for the Passover feast as usual. There was quite a large party of us travelling from Nazareth that year. My other sons went of course, and three of the wives came with some of their children. I remember my daughter did not come that year because she was soon to be confined with the birth of one of her children. I tried to enter into the holiday spirit, talking brightly with my daughters-in-law, and helping to keep the children happy and amused; but underneath, I was apprehensive and preoccupied, thinking about Jesus and the rumours of growing hostility to him and his ministry. At the same time amazing stories still abounded about his miracle-working powers. The latest was that a man who had been dead for four days had been brought back to life! Jesus' popularity had reached fever pitch on one hand, but on the other the rumbling under-current of opposition threatened to explode.

So when I heard about the tumultuous reception he received as he rode in on a donkey, I was vastly relieved, and felt my fears were unfounded. I only wished I had been there to see it!

Then I heard that he had been arrested on Thursday night. Imagine my amazement! Around midnight there had been a soft knocking on the door of the house where I had been staying. It almost went unnoticed. But John persisted and eventually someone heard and opened the door. He slipped in, found me straight away, and blurted out, 'Jesus has been arrested!'

He was panting as if he had been running, and his eyes were wide with fear. He calmed down enough to tell me about the Passover supper that Jesus and the Twelve had eaten and how they had then gone to a garden called

Gethsemane. A party of Roman soldiers had burst in and roughly accosted him and hauled him off to the palace of the High Priest. John himself had followed at a distance and gained entrance. After a brief appearance before Caiaphas, Jesus was marched off under guard to the Roman praetorium, where he now was.

I was overcome with dread. John stayed the rest of the night in the house. Neither of us slept. There was nothing we could do except wait for morning. Dawn was breaking when I went to John and implored him to find out what was happening and to come back and let me know as soon as possible.

He was gone for a long time. When he returned he had terrible news. Jesus had been shunted back and forth all night. Both Annas, the High Priest, and Caiaphas, his father-in-law, had cross-examined him. He had been dragged before a hastily convened meeting of the Sanhedrin. They had condemned him to death on the grounds of blasphemy and sent him to the Roman Governor, who in turn had sent him to King Herod. I was surprised and confused by all this activity. John thought the Jews were determined to have Jesus killed but wanted to pass the responsibility on to Rome. Pilate was clearly reluctant to embroil himself in what he saw as a local and cultural issue, so he sent Jesus back to Jewish authority, this time to King Herod, who was governor of Galilee and happened to be in Jerusalem just then. Herod was fascinated by Jesus and questioned him at some length, but Jesus said nothing. So he sent him back to Pilate.

My heart was already breaking, thinking of Jesus going through this ordeal all night with no rest, enduring lies and hatred, all alone. I longed to be able to help him in some way, but John said that there was nothing he or I or any of us could do. I wanted to go out, but John was reluctant to take me into the streets. He said the crowds were in an ugly and unpredictable mood and he did not want to expose me to danger.

Certainly there seemed to be a lot of hurrying to and fro outside and a lot of noise and shouting. Then my friend Mary, Clopas' wife, and Mary of Magdala arrived. They were weeping and distraught. We pulled them in and begged them to tell us what they knew. They had been caught up in the crowd in the square outside the praetorium and had heard Pilate offer to release to them one of two prisoners: Jesus or a convicted murderer called Barabbas. To the utter horror of the two women, the fickle crowd now seemed to have adopted Barabbas as their hero, and shouted his name.

Mary of Magdala's face was white and strained. 'I still can't take it in,' she whispered. 'Pilate called out, "What shall I do with Jesus?"'

She gulped and looked away from me. I grabbed her hand. 'What did they say?' I demanded.

'They said to crucify him,' she whispered.

She said the last two words so quietly I could hardly hear. 'What? What did you say?' I gasped.

Then she turned to me and looked me in the eye. 'Mary, they yelled, "Crucify him!" and they kept on yelling it. They chanted it together, "Crucify him! Crucify him!" Oh, Oh!' She subsided onto a chair, sobbing as if her heart would break.

I stood as one turned to stone, numb with horror. Why? Why? Crucifixion was only reserved for the worst felon, the lowest of the low, and was the most savage form of slow death that depraved minds could devise. What had he done that they should hate him so? There must be some mistake! Something had gone wrong! It could not be true. 'We must go,' I gasped. 'Quickly. Do something.' I was incoherent. I groped for some support and found I was clinging to John.

The next thing I knew was that we were all out on the street trying to get to where Jesus was. There were people everywhere, pushing and jostling and shouting. It was all so different from the happy atmosphere a few days ago when the crowd had been good-humoured. Now there was a bad-tempered, angry mood; people were surly, miserable and many were aggressively, militantly shouting and stirring up the rest to a frenzy of blood-lust.

And then I saw this tattered object, pitifully weak, stumbling up the steep stony street. A crude crown of brambles with wickedly long thorns had been crazily rammed onto his head, and tufts of beard had been pulled out, leaving raw patches. His robe was soaked with blood-stains, and over his shoulder was a huge beam of wood that weighed him down and thumped along on the ground behind him. I was looking for my son – my strong, virile, noble son. Impatiently, I strained to see if he were coming behind this poor wretched figure. I expected to see him walking calmly with his head held high, dignified in the face of this indignity, this outrageous injustice. There was still time for him to declare himself. The crowd was jeering and mocking this pitiful creature. Then, as he drew near, I realised with a sort of shocked wonder that this broken, bleeding thing, so full of pain, so tired, so beaten-up and defeated-looking was none other than my son! My Jesus!

We joined the crowd following along behind to the place of execution outside the city wall. Many just melted away, but others surged on, eager to witness the death of a blasphemer, as they thought. We were swept along, and somehow landed up at the place known as Calvary. Two crosses were already set up, with two men – thieves I afterwards found out – fastened on to them.

Surrounded by a raucous, contemptuous mob, we simply stood there, a little distance from the three crosses. I remember John holding my arm tightly and saying, 'Mary, you don't have to see this. You don't have to stay. Let me take you away.' I shook my head speechlessly. I could not look, but I could not leave.

And now the sky was thick with dark clouds, and a chill wind was whipping around. I heard the ringing clink of iron on iron, and heard the soldiers grunting and heaving as they hauled the horrible cross upright. There was a nasty 'clunk' as it fell into place in the hole dug for it. I shuddered, imagining how that must have jolted his poor battered body.

There was a lot of noise. The other two criminals were shrieking and cursing, bystanders were yelling abuse, the soldiers were shouting orders; and not far off I was grateful to see some of the women who had followed him and helped to give him meals and wash his clothes, who loved him and believed in him. They were there too, weeping as though their hearts would break.

Suddenly, above it all came a voice I knew so well. Though weak and pain-racked it carried clearly above all the hubbub. 'Father! Forgive them! They don't know what they are doing!'

That is when I began to weep, because it was so typical of him. He was always thinking of others. Immediately, I was taken back to those times when as a small boy he had been the victim of some vicious little plot and had refused to give in to self-pity. Rather than apportion blame he had pleaded for mercy for his tormentors. But once the tears had started, I couldn't stop them. The horror of it all swept over me; the unutterable pain he was enduring, the humiliation of hanging there totally exposed without a shred of clothing, the hateful jeering of the onlookers, the total indifference of the Roman soldiers callously gambling for his garments with dice, the blood, the moans from the two robbers . . . it was overwhelming, awful, unbearable.

And perhaps what was worst of all was the sting of shattered dreams, the despair of dead hopes.

Faintly I heard a conversation between Jesus and the others being crucified. One was mocking him, calling on him to save them. The other rebuked the mocker, saying that they deserved their punishment, but Jesus had done nothing wrong. Then I heard Jesus say, 'Today you will be with me in paradise.'

'At least there will be an end to this,' I thought. 'He will die and be taken out of this.'

Still I couldn't look. I pulled my veil down over my face and stood in utter misery, the tears dripping down, as scenes from his short life flashed through my mind. Those hands, once so soft and tiny which I had held and guided to hold a spoon and tie shoe-laces; that had grown strong and skilful with the lathe and chisel; that had been laid on sick people and made them well – now gashed and splintered, with big nails bashed through them. I couldn't look.

Those feet that used to kick above his head in the little crib, that ran around the paths and hillsides of Nazareth, that walked mile upon weary mile getting sore and blistered as he preached in Judea and Galilee, now also nailed and bound to the cross.

I heard him draw breath after rasping breath, struggling to get the air into his lungs that were so constricted and labouring to work in that unnatural position; so that he was continually forced to push himself up in order to suck in some air, and shudder and groan with the pressure on his tortured arms wrenched nearly out of their sockets. I tried telling myself it was all a terrible dream. This was not really happening. How could I look? I couldn't.

And still I cried under my veil. I cried for the baby I once had, the little boy, the youth, the young man – all beautiful, all lovable, all perfect. I was so heavy with grief that I could barely stand.

Into my dark misery came his voice – weaker now and at

first I wasn't sure. Then hoarsely, with a throat parched and dry, he said, 'Woman.'

John murmured to me, 'Mary, he is calling to you!' Gently he led me nearer until we were standing near that dreadful thing. Oh, how that sword was piercing my heart!

'Woman, behold your son.' The words came thickly, slowly, painfully. Then to John he said, 'Son, behold your mother.' I was speechless with wonder that at such a moment his thoughts were for me. Me! He knew that as the mother of a crucified one, I might suffer shame and loss, even destitution. Until they became believers, his unsympathetic brothers would not want to be identified with him. So he consigned me to the care of this beloved disciple.

Overcome with gratitude, I pulled the veil from my face. I looked. I looked at him on the cross. I kept on looking. And I saw, not a baby, not a man, not my son. I saw a lamb, slain as a sacrifice for sins. And I heard again the angel say, 'He shall be called Jesus for he shall save his people from their sins.' Not from Roman oppression, not from the dislocation of human affairs, not even only from their sicknesses. From their sins. A lamb, helpless, vulnerable, weak; yet innocent, unblemished, perfect. A lamb acceptable to the Holy One of Israel.

Isaiah's prophecy came with insistent clarity into my mind: 'He was led as a lamb to the slaughter, and as a sheep before its shearers is dumb, so he did not open his mouth. All we like sheep have gone astray; we have turned every one to his own way. And the Lord has laid on him the iniquity of us all.'

I could not look before because all I could see was human tragedy, pain, injustice and cruelty. But now, having looked, I could not tear my eyes away because I was beginning to see another side: God's side.

I was seeing God's answer to the sin of the world that had separated him from the objects of his love. There had to be a sacrifice. God had provided the Lamb! This was the plan. And now he was being offered up outside the city, paying for sin, even mine, that I might be reconciled to God.

I was shaken to the core. I had known his love as a son loves a mother – precious human love. But this was something that totally eclipsed it – the love of God that values individual human beings so much that he would send his only Son to die, so that whoever believes in him should not perish but receive eternal life. This was divine love.

I stood there in front of the cross, bare-headed, looking up not just at my son, but at the Saviour of the world, and light flooded my soul.

Even so, the landscape had gone strangely dark. Although it was the middle of the day, the sun was hidden, the sky grew black and a strange dread came over the watching people. They stopped their gibes and shouts. There was a subdued hush. No bird sang, no voice was heard, just the eerie rasping, gasping breathing of the victims on the crosses. I could not distinguish Jesus' face any more. In fact, soon I could not see the cross, or anything else. It was a darkness that could be felt.

I jumped as a streak of lightning momentarily lit the sky, followed by a crash of thunder. The ensuing darkness seemed thick and suffocating. Suddenly came a great heart-wrenching cry, the most terrible thing I had ever heard: 'My God, my God, why have you forsaken me?' It seemed to echo for ages in the silence that followed. In horror I shrank down on my knees, covering my face and my head. I think John was similarly overcome. How long we stayed like that I do not know, but something of vast cosmic significance was taking place. I know I felt desperately small and frightened.

Then I heard a sigh from the cross. 'I'm thirsty.' The soldiers had a jar of vinegary wine and one dipped a sponge in it, put it on a stick and held it up to Jesus' mouth. Having moistened his mouth sufficiently, he said loudly and clearly, 'It is finished!'

Then he died.

John led me away as if in a dream. I understand that the other women who were there throughout, and a rich man called Joseph (which I thought somehow fitting), were so kind as to look after the body and bury it in Joseph's own tomb.

But I went away with John. And all the while the voice of Jesus as a boy was running through my head, saying, 'Do you not know I must be doing my Father's business?' All his life and all his death he had faithfully carried out the Father's business. Now it was done.

14

A New Day

They stumbled back through the gloom to the house where they were staying. A fierce wind was blowing and rain began to lash down. They came to the door, sodden and cold right through to the depths of their beings. They entered and Mary sank down, utterly spent. There were no words to describe the anguish of the last six hours. And although Mary had received insight into why it had to be this way, and now understood that Jesus had not merely been murdered but had laid his life down for a reason, she was left with the crushing knowledge that her sin, along with that of the whole human race, had made it necessary.

The revelation of the terrible power of sin – that it should call for such an extreme remedy, that nothing less than the life of the sinless Son of God could atone for it – was overwhelming. The Lamb had died, and gone away for ever. He had done what he came to do. She could not thank him. She was left with a huge pile of grief – grief for her own personal loss of a son who had brought so much joy to her; grief that she would not see him growing on in life, that he would not be there in her old age; grief for her nation that it seemed doomed to continue without respite in oppression and bondage and that the one who could have done something about it had gone for good.

But added to this grief was a different grief. Now that she knew he was the Lamb, sacrificed for sin, such knowledge was both wonderful and terrible. To think that sin – *her* sin – had driven him to such a desperate remedy! Yes, that it had all been piled on him as he hung there that Friday afternoon. It was wonderful that he loved so much, but it was terrible that death had claimed him in the end.

He had died. Was it worth it? A supreme gesture of self-less goodwill? She supposed she would die also, eventually. How was she to know whether his sacrifice had been accepted or not? What difference did it make? All she knew was the extreme seriousness of sin and this amazing attempt at a solution. But was it lasting? As far as she could make out, nothing was certain about anyone's eternal destiny.

Later Paul would write to the Corinthians, 'If Christ has not been raised, your faith is worthless; you are still in your sins. . . .If we have hope in Christ in this life only we are of all men most to be pitied.'

If Jesus stayed dead, nothing had changed. Sin and death still reigned. Death still had a stranglehold on mankind, and people were still under the compulsion of sin. Jesus would be just another lamb. There would have to be an endless succession of lambs, stretching into eternity, unless one could be found that had the power to break the power of death.

Mary felt strangely disorientated, desolate. What was there to look forward to now? What were the consequences of this act of sacrificial love? She did not know and could not work it out. Life was dreary and meaningless and she felt very, very tired.

Daylight had long since faded into night and it was now the Sabbath. All the next day, traumatised and exhausted, she rested, feeling empty and utterly wretched. It was possibly the worst day of her life.

The next day was the first day of the week. Still drained and listless she stayed on her bed. John had gone out somewhere quite early. He came back later in the morning in a state of almost incoherent excitement, babbling about going to the garden where the tomb was, and finding it empty! Peter was with him and they had run back to the upper room where the rest of the disciples were gathered. Shortly after, Mary of Magdala had whirled in, laughing and crying and saying that she had seen Jesus alive.

John was so excited, he just had to run back and tell Mary. 'You know,' he said to her, 'it makes sense of everything. He used to say that he would rise again, but we were so lacking in understanding. I know I thought he meant that one day in the great day of the Lord we will all be raised, not realising he meant literally on the third day.'

Mary had stood up when he came in, but now she swayed, feeling faint and breathless. Concerned, John helped her to lie down again. Then, after making sure she was all right, he went to the door. 'I'm going back to the others,' he said, his face beaming with renewed hope. She heard his quick footsteps running off down the street.

She lay on the bed, watching the curtain twitching in the gentle breeze against the whitewashed wall. Her thumping heart gradually slowed to its normal rate. Could it be true? She knew it could, for 'nothing is impossible with God', as Gabriel had told her over thirty years ago. She became more and more hopeful as she sifted through her memories, pondering events and prophecies and scriptures that all pointed to one who had the power to overcome death itself. Could it be that even death could not hold him?

She got up and pottered about, mechanically performing ordinary menial tasks that were mentally undemanding, while her mind was in a turmoil. Endless questions marched through her mind. She thought of his lacerated, mangled body. If he were truly alive, what was he like now? Was he still wounded? Or was he well? Would he be substantial, or ghost-like? Where would he go? What would he do? And above all, when could she see him?

Eventually she went back to bed and drifted off to sleep. She was awakened early the next morning by John. He had brought her a drink which he now set down carefully beside her. She opened her eyes sleepily, and then seeing him there she was instantly alert. 'John! What news?'

He sat down and smiled at her, shook his head once or twice, started to speak, stopped and tried again. He seemed like a man in a dream. She touched his arm. 'John?'

He put his hand out quickly. 'I'm sorry, Mary. It's all so wonderful. I don't know where to start. Mary, I've seen him, I've seen the Lord. Last night, when we were gathered in the upper room. We were talking about everything, and there was a sudden commotion at the door and Cleopas and his friend burst in. They said they had been sadly walking home to Emmaus and someone joined them, and talked with them all the way. They said he made their hearts burn with love and understanding as he explained portions of Scripture. When they got home they invited him in. He. . . .' Here John's voice wobbled. 'He . . . oh, Mary! He broke bread and suddenly they recognised him. It was Jesus.'

Mary clutched his hand in wonder. 'John! How . . . but . . .?'

He interrupted. 'Wait, there's more. We were sitting there, in the upper room, totally amazed. . .and suddenly . . . Oh, Mary . . . him! He, Jesus. Was there. I mean . . . yes, really, it was *him*.' John's face was radiant. He sat there in a stupor, dazed, remembering.

Mary was so overcome she didn't know whether to laugh

or cry, shout or whisper, dance or faint. She did not doubt that John was speaking the truth. One glance at his face was enough to convince anyone. At first she sat absolutely still, holding her breath. Then: 'He's alive.' She whispered it to herself as if trying out a new phrase in a foreign language to see how it sounded. She said it again, only louder this time. 'He's alive! He's alive!' How good it sounded! She couldn't stop: 'He's alive! He's alive!' She got up from the bed and stretched her arms high over her head. 'Oh! He's alive!' She twirled around laughing, unable to contain her joy.

She turned a shining face to John, now nearly as incoherent as he, but composed enough to beg him to tell her all the details, but first he must go out and wait while she got properly dressed.

When he left the room she threw on her clothes with shaking hands and fumbling fingers. Then she hurried out of the room and grabbed him by the arm. 'Tell me, tell me!' she implored, whereupon John disjointedly poured out the story of how Jesus had suddenly appeared. At first they were startled out of their wits. Terrified! 'But he said, "Peace be unto you!"'

'What else?'

'He showed us his hands and his side.'

'What were they like?'

'He told us to touch him, to feel him. He was flesh and blood, Mary, not a ghost. There were big wounds in his hands and side. . . .' Again his voice trembled. 'Oh, Mary what he suffered for us! But they are healed. He is so . . . so well! He said he was hungry, so we gave him a piece of fish.' He smiled, knowing how a mother would appreciate this bit of news. 'He certainly has his appetite back!'

Mary laughed delightedly. She was pulling on her cloak and tugging him towards the door. 'Come on!' she urged.

'Why? Where are we going?'

'Wherever he is, of course!' she answered impatiently.

'But I don't know!' protested John.

'You mean you didn't find out where he is staying?' demanded Mary, frustrated.

John put his arm round her. 'No, Mary, it's not like that. I don't exactly know where he is. He just sort of comes and goes. He's the same, only. . . only different.' John struggled for words. 'You will understand when you see him. But we can't decide when that will be.' And with that she had to be content.

But she could not settle and wandered around picking things up and putting them down in a kind of dreamy daze. It was still early and she decided to go out. She was full of a restless energy and began to walk aimlessly along the street. The city was waking and the sun was up, dispersing the early morning chill. Where should she go?

'I know. I'll go to the garden, and see the tomb for myself,' she thought, and began to walk more purposefully towards the Damascus Gate, threading her way among the market-sellers already setting up their stalls and arranging their fruit and vegetables and other wares. No one took any notice of the middle-aged lady wrapped in her cloak.

She slipped through the city gate and made her way down the path outside the city wall. Not far in front of her, across the small valley, was the little hill of Calvary with all its associations of anguish. She kept her gaze resolutely away from it, and buoyed by a heart as light as her head, she rapidly came towards the garden.

It suddenly occurred to her that the gate might be locked, or soldiers might be milling about. But the gate was open and there was no one else there. She paused in the fragrant morning. The hum of the city was distant. Here in the garden was tranquillity, a few drops of dew still sparkling on the grass where the sun's rays had not yet reached, and no sounds except the rustle of leaves and the piping song of a bird.

She stood for a long time in front of the gaping cave set in the hillside. Sure enough, a great stone leaned at one side, just as John had said. The ground was trampled in front of it, with many footmarks still clearly visible in the mud, probably made by the soldiers sent to investigate the disappearance of the body. Hesitantly, she went to the entrance and, stooping, looked in. Gradually her eyes accustomed themselves to the gloom and she could discern the stone slab on which his precious body had been laid: empty now. There was no sense of 'presence' – nothing. Gone! Empty! She smiled thoughtfully and turned and groped her way out, blinking in the sunlight. Peace was in her heart, but tears were silently flowing down her face. She sat down on a nearby rock, overcome with a mixture of emotions.

A soft touch on her shoulder, a fold of linen robe brushing her face, a warm presence, breathing, living. Someone there whom she knew very well; someone strong and robust and very much alive; someone whose hand, which she now clung to, was scarred by a terrible injury but whose familiar voice was vibrant with joy and tender love. Someone whose face shone with a radiant glory that made her tremble with wonder. She slipped to her knees, pouring out her love and thankfulness, her maternal love swallowed up by her love for him as Jesus her Saviour, Son of God; and she worshipped him.

During the next six weeks, Jesus met often with his followers and explained many things about himself in the Scriptures, how Christ should suffer and rise again from the dead. He told them that repentance and forgiveness for sins should be proclaimed in his name to all nations, beginning in Jerusalem. This was the good news that Gabriel and the other angels had been proclaiming at his birth, Mary realised exultantly. Everything was coming together, making sense. 'You are witnesses of these things,' Jesus said, and she realised with a little shiver of joy that she was uniquely a witness from first to last.

He also met with James his brother, who became changed almost beyond recognition. No longer sceptical and disbelieving, he became wholeheartedly a follower of Jesus.

A few days before Pentecost, Mary and James and all her sons and scores of others who were believers were together on the Mount of Olives, receiving instructions from Jesus. He taught them many things about the kingdom of God, but on this particular day he focused their attention on someone whom he called the Holy Spirit. Of course, they had heard a little about him from the stories in the Scriptures of men in days gone by who had been empowered for special seasons and tasks by the Spirit coming upon them. Now Jesus told them that he was going to go away, but he would send the Holy Spirit to them. He would come upon them so powerfully that they would be plunged into him, and receive great authority to declare the truth about Jesus wherever they went. They were to go back to Jerusalem and wait for him to come.

They were all greatly excited by this and began to turn to each other, exclaiming, wondering when this would happen and what it would be like. Mary became conscious of feeling slightly chilly, which was unusual at that time of year, and pulled her cloak more tightly around herself. Then she saw strands of mist curling around them. She looked over to where Jesus was standing, and was startled to realise she could not see him clearly. The fog grew denser, and all around her the chatter fell silent. She clutched hold of James' hand, feeling suddenly fearful. Something odd was happening.

All eyes were now staring through the swirling mist towards Jesus. With a shock, Mary realised his feet were no longer touching the ground and he seemed to be slowly rising above them. The cloud appeared to be lifting off from the crowd and she felt the sun's warmth on her again. The space where Jesus had been standing was now empty, but high above their heads was a little puffy cloud rapidly gaining height.

The crowd stood unmoving in awestruck silence, gazing up into the sky, and they continued to gaze long after it finally disappeared.

Someone touched Mary's elbow. She looked round and saw a man she had not noticed before, dressed in a white robe. There was another one nearby. 'Where have they come from?' she wondered vaguely. The one next to her began to speak: 'Men of Galilee! Why do you stand gazing up into the sky? This Jesus who has been taken up into heaven will come back just the same way you watched him go!'

So that was it! Her suppositions were right. Jesus had gone back to where he came from. But he would return. She hoped it would be soon. Meanwhile, she was glad for him. How wonderful to be back where he belonged! What a splendid home-coming he must be enjoying!

The small crowd began to walk back down the slope towards the city. She trailed along thoughtfully. He had come, lived, died, lived again, and was gone. How quickly those thirty-odd years had passed! She wished Joseph were here now by her side to reminisce with her. Angels had announced his birth, angels had announced his resurrection. Those two men in white just now – were they angels too? If so, angels had attended his ascension to heaven as well.

She found herself recalling vividly the birth in the squalor and darkness of the stable in Bethlehem. What an entrance! What a welcome!

She wondered what he was experiencing now. 'How different it must be,' she thought wistfully. It defied imagination, but at least it must be clean, and light. Angels had sung at his birth; she was sure they sang now, filling heaven with their praises.

She smiled tenderly to herself. Words could not express her wonder and joy that she had been an essential part of the plan to reconcile man to God. Although her son had left her, she felt sure she would see him again. Her heart was strangely light; the sword had been pulled out and her wounds were healed.

15
Pentecost

Acts 2

In the upper room, 120 people gathered, including the Eleven, Mary, and the other women who had loved and served Jesus, and Jesus' own brothers. This little crowd had been with each other and with Jesus continuously now since the resurrection, drinking in everything that their Master taught them.

Now, as he had instructed, they were waiting here, praying, talking, remembering; and also attending to an important piece of business. A replacement had to be found for Judas Iscariot, the disciple who had betrayed Jesus to the authorities, and then, overburdened with guilt and shame, had hung himself. Under the leadership of Simon Peter, Matthias was chosen to take his place.

Now it was the feast day of Pentecost: the time of thanksgiving for harvest and offering of first-fruits. It was a holiday with a light-hearted atmosphere, and crowds poured into the city bringing loads of barley, wheat, grapes, figs, pomegranates, olives and honey. Jewish pilgrims of the Diaspora, speaking many different languages, filled Jerusalem.

Now in the upper room, the believers were waiting for the one Jesus had promised to send – the one he had referred to as 'the promise of the Father'. They did not know what to expect, but they were sure they would recognise him when he came.

There was a lull in the conversation. Then, faintly at first, they became aware of a roaring sound in the distance. It was like the sound of a hurricane whipping across the desert, twirling and swirling the sand-dunes like waves of the sea. The believers looked at each other, hearts pounding, awestruck as the sound increased, until the mighty roaring wind seemed to crash in on them, filling the house. Some sat as if frozen to their seats, others slipped to the floor. The roaring was all around them, engulfing them and somehow pouring into them, filling them. Mary felt as if a mighty person were there, and as this power surged around and through them, she tingled and shook. But she welcomed him. He was not a complete stranger to her, for had he not empowered her many years ago to conceive the holy life of Jesus, Son of God, and son of Mary?

Some were crying out as the power hit them. 'Oh, God!' Brightness lit the room and Mary saw that it came from leaping flames that hovered and danced over each person. She was seized with fear and wonder and uncontainable joy, and began to shout aloud praises to God – but the words were strange, a different language. Surprised, but not alarmed, she kept speaking, and the stream of words poured forth from her innermost being.

He was here again! She felt the presence of Jesus, although he was not visible in a mortal body. Now he was among them again; but not just among them, within them, making them aware of his exuberant joy, his love, his purity, and especially his power. She kept gasping, overwhelmed. This mighty Spirit was making them perceive that Jesus, whom they had known so well in measurable inches of human flesh, was actually huge, majestic, infinite and eternal . . . and yet their same dear, wonderful, accessible friend Jesus. Wave after wave of his love encompassed them – his power and presence flowing in and around them.

Mary was flooded inwardly by the Holy Spirit. The living God was near and personal! She had often heard Jesus praying and had been awed at his easy access to God, and the familiar way in which he had whispered, 'Abba, my Father.' Now her own heart was released to be able to cry out with amazed delight, and abandonment of all fear and inhibition. 'Oh, Abba, Abba!' No longer was she only a by-stander, watching the Son of God growing up in her own home. Now she felt her own relatedness, 'sonship', the inti-macy of acceptance. God was on the inside, to be known and enjoyed.

By now the room was full of noise and movement. Some were pacing up and down, faces radiant, hands waving in the air, laughing, singing, shouting; some were prostrate on the floor, drunk with glory, while others still sat in a kind of happy stupor, brokenly whispering the name of Jesus, but in a variety of languages. It was joy unspeakable and full of glory.

How long this went on she could not be sure, but at some point the room seemed too small and confined and they surged towards the door and down the stairs, spilling out onto the crowded streets, still shouting about the wonders and glories of God, but in many tongues and dialects.

The effect was sensational. People came running together from all directions when they heard the uproar, and when they saw and heard these ordinary men and women from despised, backward Galilee speaking many languages flu-ently and confidently, they were astounded.

Later, when Luke was carefully documenting the event for Theophilus, he systematically noted languages from as many as fourteen nations, sweeping round from Mesopotamia in the north-east, westward through Asia Minor, across to Greece and south to Egypt and Libya in North Africa – not forgetting Crete. The astonished crowd exclaimed in wonder that they could distinctly hear God being extolled in their own mother tongues.

'What can this mean?' they asked each other. Some rowdy elements in the crowd began to mock and yell abusively, 'Hey! They're drunk! Look at them, babbling away, behaving like a load of fools!'

Then Peter climbed up on a low wall where he could be seen, and shouted to the crowd, 'Men, fellow Jews, residents of Jerusalem! Listen carefully! Some of you are saying we're drunk. Hey! It's not yet nine o'clock! Much too early for drinking. No, we are not drunk. Now, pay attention because this is exactly what was predicted centuries ago by the prophet Joel . . .' and he went on to quote extensively from Scripture.

Mary was riveted, astounded at the transformation of this man before her very eyes. She had known him for years. He was just an ordinary fisherman from Galilee, not super-intelligent, not well-educated, and not usually very articulate. Only seven weeks ago he had been afraid to identify with Jesus and had denied he even knew him!

She listened with growing wonder as with assurance and clarity he explained to this excitable and cosmopolitan crowd that what they were witnessing was the outpouring of the Holy Spirit, exactly as the prophet Joel had foretold. He went on quickly to declare that Jesus of Nazareth had gone about doing signs and wonders, as they well knew, and God was with him. Mary caught her breath as Peter daringly asserted: 'You nailed him to a cross and murdered him!'

Not a sound came from the spellbound crowd. Peter moved on, confidently declaring that God had raised Jesus from the dead, and quoted extensively from Psalm 16 to affirm his point. He continued to preach that Jesus was the fulfilment of the prophecies of a Messiah who would inherit

David's throne, that he would die and be raised from the dead by God to sit on the throne of highest honour in heaven. He finished with a flourish: 'Let all Israel be assured of this: God has made this Jesus, whom you crucified, both Lord and Christ.'

Silence. Tense, shocked, guilt-ridden silence. Mary, glancing around her, was aware of upturned faces perturbed with a dawning understanding. If this were true, then . . . the Messiah had come and gone, and they had missed him – no, not only missed him, *killed* him! What had they done? Oh, what should they do? Here and there a sob broke out. Some covered their faces with their hands. Mary marvelled that all over the vast audience men and women were labouring under a deep awareness of guilt. Then one or two began to cry out, 'What can we do? Oh, brothers help us!' More joined in and a great wave of conviction swept across them and many now openly wept and called on God to forgive them.

With confidence and authority, Peter then explained to them that they must repent and turn from their sins and be baptised; then they too could receive the gift of the Holy Spirit. He continued preaching for a long time, explaining what came to be known as the gospel – the good news of Jesus Christ.

By the end of the day, 3,000 people were convinced and believed what Peter had said. In the following days they were all baptised, plunged beneath the waters of the Jordan or some pool or stream, to signify that they were identifying with Jesus. Symbolically they went down into death, leaving behind their old lives, and were brought up into a new life of obedience to him.

Suddenly the small group of believers had swelled to a large and significant number. Now the apostles' days were full, teaching and discipling them and forming them into the first church.

At the end of her life, Mary thought about those exciting days when it was all just beginning. Everywhere they went, the believers talked about the Lord Jesus and the new life they had found in him. Awesome days, days of miracles, and healing, many finding forgiveness from their sins, and peace of mind. That day, the Day of Pentecost, was a birthing day: the birthday of the company of the *ekklesia*, the people who had been 'called out', the church.

'My life seems to be all about births,' she confided to Luke. 'I was there at the birth of the one who came to be the Saviour, and I was there at the birth of the church – those he came to save.' She reflected for a while. 'I gave birth to one, and he now brings life to many. That reminds me of something else Jesus said: "Unless a grain of wheat falls into the ground and dies, it stays alone; but if it dies it bears much fruit."'

Watching her face now, beautiful in its serenity as she recalled those momentous days, it occurred to Luke that that maxim applied to her as well. For she also had 'died'. In that moment when she had surrendered her life and will to God, when she had said to Gabriel, 'I am the handmaid of the Lord, let it be as you have said,' she had died to her own plans and desires; she had died to her rights to organise her own life, make her decisions based on her will. But like a grain of wheat falling into the ground, she had submitted herself to being planted into the soil of God's will and purposes. The fruit that had come from that response was immeasurable and eternal.

Now the tiny sapling, the mustard seed plant that had sprung up that Pentecost day, would grow and multiply through all succeeding generations until it filled the whole earth with the glory of God.

Who Is the Queen of Heaven?

Psalm 45; 2 Corinthians 11:2; Ephesians 5:25–27; Hebrews 4:7–9; Revelation 19:6–8, 11–16

Centuries ago, a psalmist's heart bubbled over with an irrepressible desire to extol one whose excellence stirred his admiration and captivated his affection. The subject of his eloquence was a warrior king, 'fairer than the sons of men', who rode out ahead of his troops with his sword strapped upon his thigh and arrows in his hand to thrust into the heart of his enemies. But his glory and majesty lay not only in his kingly exploits on the battlefield, but in his noble qualities of 'truth, humility and righteousness'.

The psalmist's sweet song, set we are told to the tune of 'Lilies', then begins to describe a different scene. Now we are taken to a vast throne-room, where he who occupies the throne shall dispense righteous government for ever and ever. But this place, although awesome in its majesty, is also the scene of exuberant happiness, for the king and all his companions have been anointed with the oil of joy, but the king more than any of them. And the fragrance of spices and perfumes pervades the palace.

But now the king arises. Someone has entered the court, and is being led in joyful procession towards him. The king's attendants stand on tiptoe, jostling and straining to get a view of this dazzling sight. A fanfare of trumpets greets her entry, and the musicians and choristers burst into a song that rises to a crescendo as she walks with queenly dignity up the aisle towards the king. Following her is a train of women of surpassing beauty in shimmering robes of many colours; but all eyes are upon the one now approaching the throne with grace and confidence.

A blood-red carpet makes a way for her, as clothed in a glorious, gold robe, she treads slowly but surely to the steps up to the throne. The applause and the cheering is tumultuous. Does she pause here, uncertain whether to continue? Does she wait for her royal bridegroom to come down to her? Eyes now turn to look at him.

But see! He smiles at her, so welcoming, so reassuring; and he holds out his sceptre and bids her come on. So she comes serenely up the stairs and takes her place by his side. At last she is home, she is where she truly belongs – with the one she loves. This is the climax of history.

But who is she? We need to ask first, 'Who is *he*?' For although this Psalm was written in the time of King David, or his son, King Solomon, the New Testament writer to the Hebrews applies it to the Lord Jesus, and echoes of it are found all through the Scriptures. It may well have described a royal wedding back in Israel's history, but it is also, and primarily, a messianic prophecy.

It begins, as we have seen, with a lyrical description of the magnificent warrior. Gracious words pour from his lips; he rides out in splendour, wielding his sword and performing awe-inspiring deeds. The apostle John, as an old man in his nineties while imprisoned on the Isle of Patmos, had an apocalyptic vision in which he saw one riding on a white horse, who also had a sword, the word of God, and rode forth to avenge his enemies.

John heard a loud voice like the sound of many waters proclaiming, 'Hallelujah! The Lord our God the Almighty reigns. Let us rejoice and be glad, for the marriage of the Lamb has come and his bride has made herself ready!' Jesus is the King of heaven and the King is going to get married. So there will be a queen in heaven!

But who will she be? John knew Mary, Jesus' mother, very well. He did not see her being crowned as Queen of heaven. He would have recognised her. No. The one who shares the throne with the King will be the one he marries; not his mother.

But whom will the Lord marry? When John saw this vision, Mary would have long since died. John did not see her or any other identifiable individual in heaven. This is not because they are not there. On the contrary, we have many assurances that those who die in Christ will be 'for ever with the Lord'. Mary will be there and she will have her reward. But Queen of heaven? No individual shall have that honour.

John himself had asked Jesus several times if he and his brother could sit with Jesus on his right hand and his left. Jesus replied that that was not an honour he could bestow; he knew that the place was reserved for someone else: his bride.

But who shall that be? Paul wrote to the Corinthians, 'I have betrothed you to one husband, that I might present you as a chaste virgin to Christ,' and again to the Ephesians he wrote that husbands should love their wives as Christ loves the church. This is why mysteriously John saw in his revelation a holy city coming down out of heaven adorned as a bride for her husband.

The bride is not one person – she is a corporate person, a company of people who have all been redeemed, cleansed, sanctified; who have committed themselves to Jesus to honour him, love him and obey him. They are the 'called out' ones from every nation and people on the earth, who live to love him and do his will. They are the ones who await his appearing with eager longing and who will one day share his throne when he comes back to rule and reign.

Mary will not be the Queen of heaven, but she will be included in the bride as every believer will be. Jesus is waiting with passionate yearning for the day when he will claim his bride. It was in anticipation of this that he took the cup at the Last Supper and said to his disciples, who at that time were all ignorant and unaware, 'This is the last time I shall drink wine until I drink it with you in the kingdom of heaven.'

Mary is not the Queen of heaven and would have been horrified and astounded to be so designated. The glory of heaven is focused on the Lamb who is the Light. But we can see her as a type of every believer and a type of the church; one who by her response and lifestyle exemplifies what the Lord is looking for in his bride.

First of all, God initiated this train of events. He came to one who in herself had no particular reason to be selected. This is the essence of the grace of God. He sovereignly comes to whomever he will and in his kindness says to us, 'Greetings, highly favoured one!' which means, 'I welcome you, my grace is towards you, my undeserved favour is extended to you!'

Like Mary, we can be troubled by this, wondering what it is leading up to. The angel Gabriel then brought to her a message that was not new. Every Jewish girl would have known that some day, somehow, a Deliverer would come, and any girl could be his mother. But it was vague and impersonal. Now suddenly an old message became startlingly new and relevant to her. It was suddenly fresh and personal because it was addressed directly to her.

Today we preach an old message. Its contents have not changed. We believe in God sending his Son in the person of Jesus Christ, born of a virgin, to die as the sacrifice for sin.

He lived a sinless life, was crucified, dead and buried and rose from the dead to sit at the right hand of God. He is the only way by which our sin can be forgiven and we can be reconciled to God. This is the unchanging gospel, and must not be diluted to make it more palatable to modern cynical minds. But often to those modern minds, the message is archaic and irrelevant and misunderstood. Then suddenly it can confront in a way that is personal and insistent.

If you have not clearly heard the gospel before, then like Mary you can 'hear' that you are being asked to produce a holy life; and, like Mary, immediately be concerned with the utter impossibility of being able to do it. Her question was, 'How can this be, since I am a virgin?' She looked at herself and her own limitations, and knew she was powerless to do what the angel appeared to be demanding of her.

We too are totally powerless to produce the sort of life that God wants. So we ask the same question: 'How can this be, since I am uneducated? inexperienced? not "spiritual"? merely human? couldn't keep it up?' The answer is the same one that Gabriel gave to Mary: 'The Holy Spirit will come on you and the Most High will overshadow you.' The life of God can only be reproduced by God himself coming upon us. As Jesus said, we must be born again by the Holy Spirit.

What then comes to birth is holy life. It is impossible to produce holy life without him. But with him everything that he wants from us is possible, for no word of God is without power.

But one thing more was necessary – Mary's response. What would have happened if she had declined to respond to the message? I suppose that God would have found someone else to carry out his purposes. But it is unnecessary to speculate, because of course she did put aside her own agenda and embrace God's will to bring forth his Son. We honour her now for her humility and courage.

It may have seemed a bit like dying at the time. But we may be sure she did not regret her decision, because out of it came life and joy for the whole world. She proved that a life of submission and obedience to God is a life of fruitfulness. 'Whatever he says to you, do it' was to her not a choice made with gritted teeth, not a plunge into a fearful black hole, not a risk of self-annihilation, for ever wistfully looking over her shoulder to what might have been. It was a joyful exchange; his choice, his decisions, his plans instead of hers.

It was not without its pain. As Simeon had predicted, a sword pierced her heart. She ran the risk of being branded as morally loose; gave birth in squalid, unfriendly surroundings; was forced to flee to Egypt and live the life of a refugee; and then, after years of lavishing loving care on her first-born, was apparently repudiated in public. Eventually she was to witness him dying a brutal and unjust death, shamed and exposed like a common criminal.

I am grateful to her. I honour her. I think she has suffered a bad press over the centuries, being wrongly idolised by one wing of the church, but on the other hand virtually ignored by the Protestants reacting to that idolatrous stance.

I believe that although chosen for the unique honour and privilege of giving birth to the Son of God, she was still a sinful human being who was forgiven by his sacrificial death, justified by his resurrection and baptised in the Holy Spirit to enable her to be an effective witness to him.

The amazing truth is that I have just as much access to the Father and the Son as she does. I do not have to go through her as a mediator. Jesus has cleared the way for me to come boldly to the throne of grace and find mercy and grace in time of need. But I honour her, and I am grateful to God for her, because she was the channel through which his life was made available to helpless humanity.

Elijah: Anointed and Stressed

by Jeff Lucas

ELIJAH – a leader called by God, a hero of the faith, champion of God's cause, fearless opponent of the forces of evil. A man racked by self-doubt, stressed out and ready to give up.

YOU know that you have been called by God to stand for him in a slick and cynical age, to be unpopular when necessary, yet to attract people to the Christian faith. If you're honest, you're not sure how much longer you can hold it together. Let Elijah's story encourage you. Welcome to reality, where victory stems from honest appraisal, not denial.

'There is always trouble when truth is allowed to creep into Christianity. Jeff Lucas is a troublemaker and this book is excellent. Anyone involved in Christian work would do well to read it.'
– ADRIAN PLASS

'Elijah's passion and remarkable obedience to God have been captured by Jeff Lucas in this imaginative book. The combination of narrative and teaching make it hard to put down.'
– GERALD COATES

JEFF LUCAS is a speaker and Bible teacher with an international ministry. He works alongside the Pioneer Team and the Evangelical Alliance. He and his wife Kay live with their family in Chichester.

 **Kingsway Publications**

Elisha: A Sign and a Wonder

by Greg Haslam

ELISHA didn't just make pronouncements on the spiritual climate of his age – he brought about a change. He was a thermostat, not a thermometer. A man with a prophetic edge that translated into a miracle ministry.

YOU are in a society with declining values. Relationships are as polluted as the environment; commitment is seen as fanaticism. Let Elisha's story inspire you to reform society, not reflect it; to 'dig ditches' to water the land and bring revival to a thirsty nation.

'Do you need to recover your cutting edge; see that there are more with you than against you; discover that there is always enough fresh oil for you? Then bring your empty vessel to Greg's faithful and excellent exposition of these matchless stories of Elisha and you will not be disappointed.'

– TERRY VIRGO

GREG HASLAM is Pastor of the Winchester Family Church in Hampshire, where his powerful Bible exposition has helped to revolutionise the lives of many in his local community.

Kingsway Publications

Joshua: Power to Win

by Kevin Logan

JOSHUA – spied the land and saw giants. He saw things in Canaanite society to turn his blood cold and make his heart break. But he also knew what it was to overcome his fears by trusting in a God who had gone before him.

YOU – long to take a stand against the destructive forces in society today. But you also want to respond to the growing spiritual thirst of friends and neighbours. Let Joshua's story show you how.

KEVIN LOGAN is Vicar of Christ Church, Accrington, and the author of several books on the interaction of Christianity and pagan culture.

Kingsway Publications

Moses: The Making of a Leader

by Cleland Thom

MOSES began life in deep water – and there he might have stayed. But God had a unique role for him to play, and the leadership training course he devised made sure Moses was fit for that role.

YOU know that you are not yet the leader God wants you to be, but you are prepared to be trained. Let the story of Moses inspire you to a new level of dedication and service.

'Cleland Thom is a good storyteller. The early life of Moses is the story of a man taken out of useful mediocrity and shaped into a leader. If ever we needed leaders in all sections of society it is now. That is why this book is so important.'
— GERALD COATES

CLELAND THOM is a journalist and lecturer in journalism. He is also the author of *The Power to Persuade* and (with Jeff Lucas) *Friends of God*.

 **Kingsway Publications**

Samson: The Secret of Strength

by Phil Stanton

SAMSON – was a hero in his generation.
Misunderstood by his peers and by later commentators
alike, he sent out a strong ray of hope in dark times.

YOU – admire courage, but you know you need more
of it yourself. You want to stand up against the evils of
society, but the odds seem stacked against you. You
have much to learn from Samson.

PHIL STANTON is principal of Berea Bible College,
Eastbourne, and exercises a broader Bible teaching ministry.
He is the author of *Suddenly Single* and *The Bible Code – Fact
or Fake?*

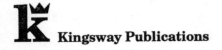 Kingsway Publications